Stella Maris Speaks

Dolphin Wisdom for a New World

Adena Tryon

Stella Maris Speaks: Dolphin Wisdom for a New World

First Edition

ISBN: 978-0-9993215-0-8 Paperback - black & white

    978-0-9993215-1-5 Paperback - full color
    978-0-9993215-2-2 Hardcover - full color
    978-0-9993215-3-9 ebook - full color

Published by Adena Tryon, LLC

Stella Maris™ visionary art is available in print and canvas at www.adenatryon.com.

Publisher's Cataloging-in-Publication Data
provided by Five Rainbows Cataloging Services

Names: Tryon, Adena, author. | Burton, Florencia, illustrator.
Title: Stella Maris speaks : dolphin wisdom for a new world / Adena Tryon ; [illustrated by] Florencia Burton.
Description: Talent, OR : Adena Tryon, 2017.
Identifiers: ISBN 978-0-9993215-0-8 (pbk., b&w) | ISBN 978-0-9993215-1-5 (pbk., color) | ISBN 978-0-9993215-2-2 (hardcover) | ISBN 978-0-9993215-3-9 (ebook)
Subjects: LCSH: Dolphins--Psychic aspects. | Angels--Miscellanea. | Feminism--Religious aspects. | Spiritual healing. | Mind and body. | BISAC: BODY, MIND & SPIRIT / Angels & Spirit Guides. | BODY, MIND & SPIRIT / Healing / Prayer & Spiritual.
Classification: LCC BF1999 .T79 2017 (print) | LCC BF1999 (ebook) | DDC 133.8--dc23.

This book is dedicated to my beloved children,
Jaden and Samara,
and to all the beautiful children.

May the majesty of your being guide our way
to a bright and blessed new world.

The Gift

I have left a shell for you
A gift from my heart to yours
Given and received instantaneously
Beyond time and space

Place it against your ear to restore your inner hearing
Hold it to your eyes to activate your visionary sight
Kiss it gently tasting the seawater upon your lips
Empowering your true voice

Deeply inhale the fragrant ocean breeze
Holding the shell gently upon your heart
Listening to the sound of your ancient and steady beat
The beautiful drum of your soul
Stirring memories of distant times and long forgotten places
So you may remember who you are and why you have come

Receive the gift of your star heart essence
Your Divine Self
Washing you in waves of liquid light

Remember
Now and always
To rest in the realm of your light
The ocean of oneness

We are united once more
A-Ju-La
One Family
One Being
One Light
One Heart
One Love

Adena

Contents

Part 2
Love Messages from Stella Maris

Part 3
Light Messages and Activations from Stella Maris

Embrace Child Power
Stella Maris Children Messengers:
Kaleosi, Luz, Lolli, Ra, Phaedra, and Ama

Stella Maris Adult Messengers and Queen A'Mara:
Theseus, Mahadra, Grandmother Izoma and
Grandfather Skylan, Kelti, and Drahana

Part 4
Final Reflections

Acknowledgments

With overflowing gratitude to the angels, seen and unseen, who lift my life with their wings of beauty and grace.

To the Divine Mother of all Life: Thank you for your loving presence in my life. It is an honor to live my life as a prayer for your great work on Gaia Earth. May all beings be blessed to know you as their own sacred hearts.

To Stella Maris: Thank you for the opportunity to share your messages. Your blessings have profoundly changed my life. Your gift of the Beauty Way is the way I choose to live forevermore. You have brought everyday magic back to my life, and I am grateful for your vibrations of joy, play, laughter, and fun! I am so grateful to know you are here with me in every moment. Not to mention how you activated my writing gifts for all the future books to come.

To all of my Guides, Angels, Ascended Masters, and Star Family: Thank you for your incredible support. You have always led me to the right place at the right time and given me the courage to follow my heart. Thank you for the brilliance of your higher realm guidance and wisdom.

To the Dolphins: Thank you for anchoring unity consciousness on Earth and for being our guides and dear family on Gaia Earth. May you be remembered and loved as our loving 'aumakua. May you always have the protection and peace you deserve. May humans understand the infinite wisdom and unconditional love that you embody here.

To James: You are the love of my life. Thank you for your incredible support and love. I am so blessed to have you as my evolutionary partner. May you always know the depth of my love for you and the pivotal role you have played in the emergence of this book and the many ways you have blessed my life. Your love has healed me so deeply, and I am grateful to share the journey of this life together.

To Jaden and Samara: My beloved children, you are my heart walking in human form. You are the greatest gifts of my life, and your presence inspires me daily. Thank you for giving me the time and space to write this book and for understanding my life purpose so brilliantly. Your shining smiles and excited faces gave me the love fuel to continue. You believed in me, even when I didn't believe in myself. Your support has meant the world to me. I love you, beautiful Starseed Imagineers. Thank you for the light and wisdom I see within your eyes. Thank you for coming here at this time; you are a divine blessing to the entire world.

To Mom and Dad: Thank you for the gift of my life and for raising me with a spiritual basis. You are rare and beautiful people who have blessed me with many opportunities for learning. Thank you for your support. I love you.

To Anne and Larry: Thank you for your wonderful love and support. You are living inspirations, and I knew I could tell you about this book first because of your extraordinarily open minds and hearts. Thank you for giving me the greatest gift—James. I am so grateful for your presence in my life.

To Suni: Thank you for always standing by me with love and encouragement. Your friendship and support has always meant the world to me. We have shared our lives together for the past eighteen years: our careers, the births of our children, and all of the important events in between. It has been my greatest joy to share my life with my bestie. You have given me the courage to stand as my true self and believed in me from the beginning.

To Maria: Thank you for your partnership and friendship on this Beauty Way path. Your presence in my life is such a gift. Sending you infinite blessings and gratitude for walking together in our most beautiful lives.

To Chelsea: Thank you for being my cheerleader and true friend. You always encouraged me, and your support means the world to me. May you always know the beauty of your heart and gifts as a divine priestess.

To my Solstar Companions: I dedicate this book to you, all of the sentient being light activators who have graced my life with your love. You made my existence here possible, through the power of your pure hearts and light. Thank you to my many tree and flower companions and to the crystal people. Blessings to my invisible mystical animal companions and fairy beings.

To Gaia Earth: Thank you for providing a wonderful home for us to grow spiritually. One of my deepest prayers is for your healing and that your body may be restored through the power of unity consciousness and the divine feminine. You have given us the rare opportunity to live and evolve here. May we show our love for you through the actions we take on your behalf. May you now receive the many blessings you have given us returned to you one thousandfold.

To my Soul Sister Florencia Burton: Thank you for saying yes to the creation of the visionary art for this book. You were the first to confirm the existence of Stella Maris, and I will always be grateful. It has been an honor to partner with you, my true sister of my heart.

To Susan Casey: Thank you for the awareness you created through your book *Voices in the Ocean*. Your book was the only one Stella Maris guided me to read while I was writing this book. It was beautifully written and inspiring. I highly recommend your book as a resource to understand the dolphins in new ways.

To Jean Houston: You are one of my greatest inspirations. Your profound work has paved the way for so many others. Thank you for being a forerunner and for making the way easier for me. You are a true divine feminine leader and role model.

To Claire Zammit and Katherine Woodward Thomas: Thank you for the gift of Feminine Power Mastery. The principles I learned from you have activated my gifts and helped me to step into my highest divine service.

To Tosha Silver: Thank you for giving me practical ways to align with the Divine through the power of prayer. Your books helped me to create everyday miracles and step into my Higher Self.

To Betsy Rapoport: Thank you for your open mind and heart. You are such a gift to this world. Your help as developmental editor was incredibly valuable, and I honor your insight and wisdom deeply. Infinite blessings to you.

To Aaron and Violet: Thank you for helping to bring *Stella Maris Speaks* into its physical form and for assisting with its birth into the world. You are incredible light beings, and co-creating with you was a joy and honor! Infinite dolphin blessings to you.

Part 1
Introducing Stella Maris

Chapter 1
The Great Leap

Without knowing how, without knowing why, I leap, I love, I fly.

I am sitting on the edge of a boat, gripped by fear. My legs dangle awkwardly, fins barely touching the sapphire-blue water. The Bay of Banderas slowly reveals the presence of mysterious wild creatures. "Jump!" a loud voice shouts from behind me, as I entertain thoughts of my certain death. Why, oh why, did I decide to do this?

"Jump!" commands the voice once more. Inhaling deeply, I gather all of my courage and leap into the ocean water, hoping I will survive to tell the tale. As my body makes contact with the water, a long-forgotten memory surfaces. I witness a luminous figure approaching me in the turquoise water of a vast ocean. She looks at me with love, her round dolphin head emitting radiant white light, her translucent heart sending waves of joy, as if I am her long-lost best friend. My heart leaps in response, sending her love in return. Our connection feels transcendent and eternal. A flash of light brings a second vision, a dream where I swim with angelic dolphins of light, effortlessly breathing underwater and delighting in the warmth of the Ocean Mother. We play, leaping and jumping with our whale friends. The dolphins show me undersea villages, sacred temples, and other beautiful places. The underwater world is so familiar and peaceful . . .

The cold Pacific water shocks me back into my body and current reality. Oh yes, I am drifting in the open ocean with wild dolphins, the "tigers of the sea," according to our biologist guide. I tense with anticipation of their sudden underwater presence. The visibility is poor and I can see only about six inches in front of me. My fear surges. "What the H-E double hockey sticks am I doing?" I calm myself by taking several deep breaths, carefully placing my snorkel over my face and drifting through the water.

Suddenly, a baby dolphin darts six inches in front of me. "Eek, garg!" I bellow through my watery mouthpiece. I glance below the water, seeing a curious three-foot baby dolphin carefully returning for a closer look. Darting by with surprising quickness, her loving eyes gaze at me like I'm a fascinating science project. I admit I probably look pretty strange in this weird snorkel gear.

I hear a high whispering voice: *I am Kaleosi.* The voice startles me, and I suck in a mouthful of sea water. After clearing my snorkel, I look under the water again. The baby dolphin has brought back her mother and several other pod members, who all gaze at me with the same wonder. In their presence, I am overcome with peace and a calm surrender. My heart bursts with joy and love. They gather close, all around me, encircling and blessing me. Some of the dolphins descend deep below my body, and I hear their sonar and clicks, as ripples of healing sound waves rise through the water and land on my skin. A mix of sheer excitement and fear makes my heart beat fast. I know something wonderful and unexpected is happening.

The strong current brings me to a point of exhaustion; I simply can't keep up with these agile swimmers. It is no use to swim after them—they are too fast. I must wait for them to choose to come to me, and they do! Returning again and again, they swim so close I can reach out and touch them, but I keep my hands to myself, as our guide instructed.

When it is time for me to leave the water, I telepathically communicate to them: *Thank you. I'll be back, dear friends!* What a gift I have been given by these wild beings. A huge smile explodes across my face, and a deep sense of awe fills my being. What joy, what beauty! I am fascinated by their interest in connecting with me and the feeling of mutual recognition that I just can't shake. I gaze at the pod longingly, as they disappear under the ocean. I vow to return to the dolphins as soon as I can, and I notice my body feels heavy and awkward in the dry air. There is a distinct feeling that I was created to live in the water too.

When I return to my condo, I immediately sit down to write about my experience so I won't forget even the tiniest detail. As I begin writing, the same high, watery dolphin voice returns: *I am Kaleosi, and my name means "pure voice calling." I reach out to you beyond all forms, space, and time.* I blink to clear my head, noting I am alone in my room. Standing and shaking my body, I take several deep breaths. What is happening? The disembodied voice continues: *My sound and vibration hold the pure essence of your heart. Your heart is your guide for the planetary changes to come.*

All right then, clearly I'm dreaming. I walk to the bathroom mirror and tap my cheeks hard, leaving red marks. My rational self implores me to wake up and get a grip on reality. *There is just no way this is happening,* my logical left brain protests. Another part of me rises, speaking confidently to my worry brain. *You are a perfectly sane and grounded person. You are not going crazy. In fact, you worked in the mental health field for the past seventeen years, so you are very familiar with the symptoms of a psychological break, and I can assure you this is not one.*

Have you ever embraced an inexplicable moment when you knew your life would change forever? This is where I stood, teetering on the edge of ordinary life and an unknown abyss. A revolutionary idea began to take form in my mind, emerging like a bright blue butterfly from a chrysalis. *Something extraordinary happened when I was with the wild dolphins . . . but what? Something beyond the ordinary. . . . Something mystical. . . . The swimming-immersive experience seemed to have opened a doorway between my consciousness and the consciousness of the dolphins. Was this even possible?*

A deep knowing replaced my worry, as an ancient memory stirred. The doorway to my psyche opened, allowing the amnesia of this life to dissolve ever so slightly. I curiously peered beyond the veil. This dolphin communication was familiar. A vision unfurled like the petals of a pink lotus. I witnessed myself standing next to the aqua-blue sea, a white marble open-aired temple behind me. A long white dress flowed around my body, as I gazed toward the water. Dolphins arrived at the shoreline, greeting me. Pure joy surged through me, as I witnessed our genuine affinity and telepathic communication. Ah yes, this is familiar, and I have missed this connection so deeply.

With a sudden jolt, I am back in my Mexican condo. The clarity of my vision is a revelation! I must remember more. My mind decides it's time to pitch an extreme fit, bellowing negative thoughts at me in disbelief. I anchor myself in a place of peace, acknowledging my mind's tantrum, and I kindly ask it to step aside for just a moment, motioning to a nearby chair. I imagine my rational left brain waddling over to the chair and taking a seat, with a pouty look. Glowering at me from the corner, it accepts my decision to listen to my heart.

Returning to my writing, I carefully listen to the voice of Kaleosi, scribing every word of her first message. The words appear in my mind's eye and flow through my pen onto the page. *You are a volunteer. You have simply forgotten who you are. You are here to awaken the new age of peace on Earth. Remember who you are and why you have come. You are here to hold the vision of what can come, not to become disheartened by what currently is.*

Difficult memories of childhood flood my consciousness. Always feeling different, wondering if I belonged, my outrage at the way humans treated each other and the Earth, it all made sense now. *I am a volunteer.* I repeat this out loud several times, to integrate her message more fully. For most of my life, I believed something was wrong with me because I didn't fit in, and now Kaleosi was revealing a new truth to me: *It wasn't that something was wrong with me, something was wrong with the modern world, and I was here to help.* How I wished I could have known this sooner! It would have saved me so much heartache and self-doubt as a child. My entire life flashed before my eyes: my connection to children, my profession as a social worker, rescuing animals, assisting the homeless, helping the dying. I had always lived with a constant drive to help.

Kaleosi continued: *I am a Light Messenger. A light messenger is an angel sent by the Source to support and help other beings. We call the Source the Divine Mother. Light messengers can be in both physical and spirit form, as we wish. You are a light activator. A light activator is a light worker volunteer who has chosen to be born at this moment to initiate a new age of peace on Gaia Earth. Some use the words "light worker" to describe these humans. We prefer to use the words "light activator" because it describes your illuminating action, and is more fun than being a "worker." All light activators are here to bring light and love for the healing and awakening of all beings, and they can appear in human and nonhuman forms. In this time, we are all here to help with the gigantic amount of healing that needs to occur here. We are here to work together.*

Kaleosi used the name "Starseed" to refer to all beings who are seeding, growing, and blooming a new consciousness on Earth through the starlight gifts embedded in their hearts. She showed me a vision of a person as a five-pointed star, light spokes shining out from their heart, highlighted by angelic glow and sparkles.

She used many words I was not familiar with, but I trusted I was hearing them correctly. When I was confused, I simply asked her for a definition. So don't worry if the words or terms in this book are new to you—they are new to Earth! I put a Stella Maris Glossary section at the end of the book to help you understand the words and terms more fully.

1: The Great Leap

Kaleosi spoke: *This is just the beginning of a wonderful change, and there is great hope for Gaia Earth's future. You will witness everyday miracles beyond your comprehension in this lifetime. You are a light activator, here to anchor love and light. We are here to support you. Will you help us by sharing our messages through your heart, voice, and hands? Will you tell everyone we are here?*

As you might imagine, I was trying really hard to take this in. I became still, so still you would have wondered if I was breathing. The communication was so clear, and I knew this was real, more real than my so-called regular life. I pondered the greatness of the invitation, knowing it was beyond my mind's understanding. My heart was the only way to answer this call. Doubt slowly crept its way back in. *Is this my imagination, or am I really communicating with dolphin light beings? Was I really connected to dolphin consciousness?*

There was only one way to find out: to accept their invitation. My heart spoke with lightning clarity. "YES!" I exclaimed out loud. "I will help you." The loudness of my voice echoed back at me, disturbing the silence of my room and causing me to jump slightly. The power of my words sent a rush of joy and anticipation through my body, for I knew in my bones that my life would never be the same.

I imagined myself leaping off into the unknown, jumping from a high cliff into the white mist, thrilled, terrified, and smiling from ear to ear. Trusting the guidance of my heart, I jumped with faith, knowing the arms of the Divine Mother would catch me. So I dove into unity, joyfully falling into the ocean of light, returning to my dolphin family and the great mystery Herself.

It is more important than ever to call on higher-realm support that is always available for your life. One of the easiest ways to connect to your helpers is to know the names and symbols of the higher realm beings you are calling on. We, Stella Maris, share our names now so you will have an easy way to call on us for assistance. Using our sacred names instantly connects you with us in the higher vibrational realms. We are here to assist you in creating your unique Beauty Way life by helping you anchor the energies of love and light in your form. We invite you to call on us often! —Stella Maris

Chapter 2

The Creation of This Book

Diving into the Higher Realms 101

You are still here; great news! I am going to pause my story for a moment to review a few of the concepts used by Stella Maris so you will understand their messages better. Stella Maris says they are communicating to us from the higher realms. You may be wondering, where and what are these "higher realms"? There are many worlds and realms that coexist with ours in different energetic frequencies. Joy and love permeate higher vibrational worlds, where the power of the light is more evident and life exists with more ease. The higher realms are like heaven or paradise, because the Source of universal love energy is known and infuses everything at all times. The Divine Mother Source offers the purest love in the universe. Light messengers or angels live in this oneness and can awaken this love more fully in you. These realms coexist with our world. Physicists are now discovering proof of the many dimensions and realities in our multi-mysterious universe.

Who exists in the higher realms? The Divine Mother Source of all life exists as everything and all beings. There is also a multitude of beings: angels, ascended masters, soul guides, passed loved ones, and other light helpers. The word "angel" literally translates into "light messenger," so these two terms can be used interchangeably. You have a specially appointed team of soul guides, guardian angels, and ascended masters. Soul guides can be animals, star beings, and loved ones who have passed on, continuing to exist on the other side of the veil. Ascended masters are spiritual teachers who once lived on the Earth and are now available in spirit form to offer guidance.

Your unseen helpers respect your free will, and they will not interfere with your choices unless you invite them to do so. They are thrilled to help, but always must be asked first. One of those universal laws! You can ask for guidance and help from the angels and ascended masters at any time by simply asking for them out loud or quietly within yourself. My circle of light fills me with immeasurable love and support.

This is a challenging human journey; why wouldn't you be given an incredible team to be at your side? As you develop more of your truly human abilities and learn how to ask for help, you can access your guides, angels, and helpers more easily. And don't forget to ask your Higher Self as well. This divine part of you is so important as a guide for your life.

What is the Higher Self? It is a term to describe the part of you that is true, eternal, divine, and conscious. Your God self, your real and authentic self. Your heart. This is the part of you that exists eternally. It is the energy you are made of, the one Source who lives and creates everything. You are literally living divinity in human form! Have you heard the saying "you are in this world but not of this world"? The Higher Self is what this revelation is referring to. Your Higher Self always resides in the realm of unity consciousness and can be accessed more and more as a guiding force for your life.

Most people receive intuitive messages all of the time, but our modern-day culture teaches you to ignore or discard them as not real. I can assure you, they are real, and using your natural abilities is easier than you think. Pay attention to all you are perceiving, and you may be surprised by the messages you receive. And by the way, when did your imagination get such a bad rap? Slowly but surely our culture teaches us to close off from these perceptions, and that our imagination is useless and unreal. Your imagination is one of your most powerful tools for creation. It grants you access to the vast intelligence of the Source through the power of your Higher Self. Your human eyes see a small spectrum of light and your human ears hear only a narrow range of sound. The invisible Source realm is vast, and you can only experience it through your Higher Self, heart, intuition, and aligned brain. Multidimensional perception is a gift we are all given.

Now that you have had my mini-course, Higher Realms 101, let's get back to my discovery of Stella Maris.

The Writing

Upon returning home, I created a commitment ceremony to make my dedication to helping Stella Maris official! I gathered a bowl of water, small dolphin figures, crystals, and flowers to make a circular altar next to a bright blue delphinium in my garden. I proclaimed my commitment out loud through a spontaneous ceremony guided by my Higher Self. When I was finished, I sat still and listened. There was a flurry of voices, and I quickly grabbed my paper to write down the messages I was receiving. It was an avalanche of words, visions, sounds—the information flowed like a waterfall in and through me.

We are Stella Maris, light messengers who are here to serve humanity as a high council of the Divine Mother, the Source of all life. There are many different names for the same creator being from which we all arise. We like to call the Source the Divine Mother or the Maha Ocean Mother. The Divine Mother is always here; her beautiful presence is the One in which all life is created and expressed. Recently, your world has forgotten the Divine Mother, and thus your own true identity and nature. We are here to help you to remember, to intervene on behalf of all life, to restore balance and peace to the world.

Our name, Stella Maris, means "Starlights of the Sea." We are starlight messengers from the higher realms who have formed a high council to assist the world. A high council is a group of light messengers and ascended masters who gather as a group to offer their support and guidance. We are dolphins who work with the divine feminine teachers Mother Mary, Quan Yin, and Queen A'Mara, to support your awakening and healing.

Twelve different dolphin light messengers introduced themselves to me by name. I could hardly keep up, writing down the unusual and interesting names. I asked them, why so many names?

We give you our names so you can call on us whenever you like. Instead of saying, "Hey, dolphins," which is pretty general, you can call us by our true names, which instantly bring us to you. The name Stella Maris is important because it tells the world our unique identity and purpose as starlight messengers from the universal sea of unity consciousness. Our individual names hold the resonance of our divine qualities and unique identities. Each name carries a vibration of sound, a star wave of healing light. This makes it easy for you to call on each of us for support when you are experiencing different challenges and to receive our blessings instantly.

As I sat in the garden, the Stella Maris dolphins circled around me, creating a spinning vortex of invisible water. They blessed me one by one with symbols of color, light, and sound. All three divine feminine masters embraced me, lifting me into a space filled with bright ivory light, where I rested beyond time and space. After some time, I returned to my body in a new way, filled with unspeakable joy for my new life purpose, to share their messages.

To this day, I still experience Stella Maris's presence in this way. White light and flowing aqua water fills the space around me as I am surrounded by joyful angelic dolphin beings who swim, jump, and dive. They like to swim in circles, creating a spinning vortex, a portal to the higher realms of our being. Emanating playful laughter that sounds like beautiful bells, their clicks and sonar sounds come and go in different successions.

I committed to write each day, choosing two places for my task: outside in the garden or inside my meditation room. Before writing, I centered myself and called Stella Maris by name through the recitation of the prayer they gave me. Sometimes I experienced incredible resistance to my divine assignment. I showed up anyway. One of our greatest fears can be the infinite power of our creativity, genius, and greatness. Plus, the fear of the unknown. My fear was great and my ego self had many unhappy feelings about my new passion and purpose. I honored all of my feelings while remaining committed to the guidance of my heart.

In the beginning there was a nicely organized pattern of mutual communication, but then everything changed. Just when I became comfortable receiving their messages, Stella Maris began visiting me twenty-four hours a day. They showed up in my dreams, first thing in the morning, and at night. All bets were off; it was a twenty-four/seven affair. Ideas, messages, and even specific suggestions like what to look up online were communicated to me all of the time. I would hurriedly grab a piece of scrap paper and jot down notes as quickly as I could. I began carrying around a small notebook, so I would be ready to receive messages at any moment. By the way, I am not a morning person, so it was not uncommon for me to grumble when their cheery energy showed up in the wee hours of the daylight. Sometimes I told them to wait or to come back later. Each messenger was kind and respectful, but also very excited, and unbound by the constraints of embodied earthly life. I was even shown photographic images of the pages in this book, highlighting exactly where I needed to add information or make changes.

Knowing their individual names helped me track who was speaking and what they were sharing. Each messenger had my full and undivided attention. As we worked together, I noticed a clearing of my psychic channels. It happened quite naturally through the receiving of their messages and through the powerful healing of their guided visionary meditations. Now I could hear, see, feel, and know with crystal clarity. When I wrote, time stood still. Deeply immersed in the creative process, my individual self dissolved in oneness.

Day after day, I sat in front of my computer, having no idea of what I would write. No plan, no figuring out, no way of knowing. My critical left brain persisted with its angry tantrums: *How can I figure this out? What's the plan, where is the outline? This isn't real; it's just your imagination!* My logical left brain and intuitive right brain were engaged in an epic battle. Left brain versus right, masculine versus feminine, thoughts versus heart, Earth-based reality versus heavenly realms, inner critic versus inner wise woman. When the battle escalated, I took a deep breath, placing my hand on my heart. This was the way I connected to the divine drum beating within, my trusty honing device and north star that always resided at the center of my being. I deliberately placed my trust and faith in my Higher Self, the part of me that is divine, holy, and eternal.

Then the words flowed naturally, spinning through the cosmos and through my being. I learned to speak the messages aloud so I could fully immerse myself in the experience, a modern-day woman channeling as the ancient oracles did. Channeled writing was not something I was very familiar with when I began writing for Stella Maris. I was surprised by the messages that were coming through me. Many questions arose within my mind. Is the source of the writing my Higher Self? *Yes.* Are these light dolphins real? *Yes.* I struggled to make sense of the experience, an intricate weaving of my innate wisdom, my God self, and communication from dolphin consciousness. It became clear that I was tapping into a universal intelligence or unity consciousness, where Stella Maris exists all of the time. Miraculously, words appeared on my pages, day after day, and after three months I had written 150 pages.

When I had doubts, Theseus, an elder dolphin of Stella Maris, directed me to look up other famous people who have channeled wisdom for the greater good, including Abraham Lincoln, Rudolf Steiner, Nikola Tesla, Pythagoras, Rumi, Jesus, and Anaïs Ninn. Theseus spoke to me about the universal source, that we all have the capacity to tap into and receive the gifts of divine guidance and knowledge, creativity, and inspiration. I also like to call the Source the Divine Mother, but you can call the Source whatever you like—God, Creator, or Love. I use the name Divine Mother because it aligns with how I experience the Source as an immense and loving presence. Unity consciousness exists beyond the definition of male or female; it is simply the Source, and I believe everyone has the ability to connect to this one true energy of all life. This vast Source of love and divine intelligence is always available to us, and it loves us more than we can imagine! One of my biggest leaps was trusting in the process and the guidance I was receiving. Making the leap of faith day in and day out, I was living with extreme vulnerability, on the edge of the unknown, holding hands with my fear daily. No figuring out, no knowing, no plan, no understanding. Yes flowing, yes listening, yes being, yes receiving. This is how I navigated the divine feminine path of creating this book.

In consenting to leave my normal life behind, I walked through the open doorway of the great mystery with Stella Maris. Everyday miracles began to appear, synchronicities beyond belief, and my faith was confirmed. I believe all of this was possible because of my biggest prayer: to align with my Higher Self, in highest divine service, and to live my divinity. These prayers infused my life with harmony, and I experienced a beautiful and intimate connection with life itself. Everything around me had a voice, speaking to me through the field of oneness. The redwood trees, dragonflies, and rocks all communicated their divine songs. It was one dance of many forms, one breath, one being.

For nine months, I listened, wrote, and journeyed with Stella Maris, receiving their divine initiations, messages, and activation blessings. The irony is not lost on me that this time frame is exactly how long it takes to develop a human baby within the womb. I was actively nurturing and growing a divine book baby. Soaking up the teachings of Stella Maris like a thirsty desert flower, I realized the book was writing me, instead of me writing it. The teachings and activations literally redesigned the energy in my body, my awareness of who I was, and directed my new Beauty Way of life. There were great highs and the lowest lows as I released my human patterns of suffering and consented to live more and more in the spaciousness freedom of my light.

The Stella Maris Visionary Art

Finding Florencia Burton is a great example of how everyday miracles began to appear in my life. Stella Maris told me from the very beginning that art would be an important part of their messages. Browsing art online, I came across one of Florencia's images: three dolphins swimming in a circle around a six-sided flower of life. Her art transmitted the same energy as Stella Maris's messages.

I wrote to ask if I could place this image in my book. She responded with a resounding *yes* and asked to "know more about the book being born of my hands." Our frequent emails soon revealed a soul connection that transcended time and space. She lived in Argentina and I lived in the United States, and we spoke different languages. Inexplicably, we understood each other perfectly. She too had experienced the presence of Stella Maris and was the first person in the outer world to confirm their presence to me. I wept with gratitude and reassurance, taking comfort in knowing someone else shared this connection. Running around my house crying, I shouted, "This is real, this really is real!" My rational brain could not account for the great alignment between us, and I was delighted by the deep magic our alliance created. It was uplifting and inspiring. As I wrote, Florencia created the perfect art, illustrating the messages I was receiving, without a word of communication between us! It was miraculous!

Florencia is a self-taught artist who creates through the power of her intuition and imagination. She often begins with a blank page and allows the art to emerge on its own, discovering what appears. The Stella Maris visionary art transmits healing through imagery and light language, a universal heart language we all understand at a soul level. Light language is beyond words; it holds an energetic transmission through its waves of light.

Stella Maris's wisdom is communicated here through art, words, and symbols that hold the vibration of joy, love, and light. Light and love are the antidote and divine feminine medicine for living in this traumatizing time on Earth. We are living in a time of great miracles, when heaven is intervening on Earth, but it can appear very dark before the light. The Divine Mother is intervening in our lifetime for the good of all beings. When I meditate with Stella Maris's words and their visionary art, I experience a powerful transmission of light energy. They told me from the beginning that art would be an essential part of their communication, and I am so grateful to Florencia for her beautiful contribution.

Chapter 3
The World of Stella Maris

Meet Stella Maris

Stella Maris are dolphin light messengers who work in service to the Divine Mother Source. They are here to assist us with personal and planetary healing. The name Stella Maris means "Starlights of the Sea," "Guiding Spirits of the Sea," and "Divine Feminine Protectors." Their name reveals information about their identity, signifying their role as divine feminine teachers and healers of the highest order. Light messengers are like angels and can appear in physical and nonphysical forms.

A high council is a group of ascended masters, guides, and light messengers who offer you support as friends, teachers, guides, and allies. Stella Maris has created the Stella Maris High Council, which includes the pod of Stella Maris, ascended masters Mother Mary and Quan Yin, and divine feminine teacher Queen A'Mara.

Ascended masters are different from light messengers. They are spiritual teachers who awakened to their divinity through human life and often create teachings on Earth. After a human life, they ascended to the higher realms, where they offer help and guidance to all beings.

As light messengers, Stella Maris can exist in both physical and spiritual forms. They are always connected to dolphins on Earth through their shared unity consciousness. Sometimes they may even choose to take the physical form of a dolphin. At first, I thought I was experiencing interspecies communication, but I quickly realized the Stella Maris dolphins existed beyond mere physical reality as incredible multidimensional beings. How else was it possible for them to communicate to me beyond space and time? They even have the ability to shape-shift, appearing as dolphins, angels, and sometimes even humans.

Are the Stella Maris dolphins in physical form on Earth? *Yes.* Are they existing in the unseen energetic realm as light messengers? *Yes!* I know, it's pretty darn confusing, but maybe we are not supposed to understand the mysteries of life. Let's just say you can't really wrap the left brain around how multidimensional they really are. The universe is quite a mystery, with many levels of consciousness and dimensions. I have become increasingly comfortable in not-knowing or not understanding! I truly can't figure it out, and in the end, it doesn't matter. What matters most is that you know they are here and always available to help.

Dolphins as Our 'Aumakua

'Aumākua are intimate members of the human family, spiritual relationships with them are especially close and their presence is sought for feast and festivity, as well as in time of crisis. They act as healers and advisors. —J. Gutmanis

Stella Maris speaks of their role as our *'aumakua*, a word from Hawaiian spirituality that means guiding ancestor or ancient family. The Hawaiians believe the 'aumakua are guides that can intervene to help us. The appearance of an animal who was an 'aumakua is believed to be a good omen and there are many stories of how these guides saved descendants from harm. 'Aumakua help through their inspiration, protection, and guidance, existing in the higher realm and taking forms of their choosing on Gaia Earth.

The Hawaiian word for dolphins is *nai'a,* which translates to the energy of unconditional love. This is what I feel most from Stella Maris. They enfold me in waves of a deep and abiding love as a dear family member. Within this context, the name Stella Maris makes so much sense. They truly are our "Guiding Spirits of the Sea" and "Divine Feminine Protectors" who support us as our ancient family.

The Science

Stella Maris would like me to briefly share scientific information about dolphins and the Divine Mother field to satiate your mind. Hopefully, this will allow your left brain to step aside, allowing your heart to fully receive their messages.

Dolphins and Humans Are Closely Related

While I was writing the messages from Stella Maris, I chose not to read any other writings about dolphins, especially channeled dolphin messages. I wanted to hear the messages most clearly without the influence of others. There was only one book Stella Maris insisted that I read: *Voices in the Ocean,* by Susan Casey. This beautiful book explores the human/dolphin connection and the plight of dolphins in modern times. The science I share here is found in Susan Casey's book (which I highly recommend) and from a presentation I attended at Wildlife Connections in Mexico.

Humans and dolphins are both mammals who breathe air, nurse their young, and communicate through complicated language. Dolphins have five-fingered hands within their flippers. I was stunned when I first viewed the skeleton of a dolphin fin in Mexico; it looked just like a human hand. Dolphins are highly evolved beings with advanced brain capacity and underwater skills that give them the nickname the "tigers of the sea." Even sharks are intimidated by dolphins, according to my biologist guide. Yet dolphins rarely, if ever, harm humans. Why? There seems to be a longstanding kinship or recognition between dolphins and humans that defies logic. This connection is reflected in many world culture myths and stories.

It is estimated that dolphins have been on the Earth for 95 million years. Science shows that humans and dolphins have strikingly similar DNA. Dolphin brains are actually larger and more advanced than human brains, and they can hear sounds eight times higher than we do. They use a very advanced form of echolocation and can literally "see" through their hearing by using their sonar to produce a type of X-ray vision. Dolphins are even aware of magnetic fields that we cannot perceive.

Dolphins have perfectly designed hydrodynamic bodies that glide through the water with incredible power and speed. Unlike humans, dolphins consciously breathe, rising to the surface to inhale. If a dolphin passes out, their pod members will notice and lift them to the surface for air. Dolphins have a seamless connection between their right and left brain hemispheres, and sleep by resting in one hemisphere or the other, staying awake at all times. Like humans, dolphins have highly advanced societies. They have individual names, an awareness of their own identity, and highly developed capacities for empathy, intuition, and communication. Although they know themselves as individuals, they are highly connected to their pod and seem to operate as a collective "we." Dolphins develop long-term relationships and recognize each other after long periods of time apart. Dolphins will stay with their pod, never abandoning their community members, even if it means they will be harmed or killed.

We are only just discovering the capacity and presence of these amazing creatures. May we recognize dolphins as our family and honor their right to life, freedom, and a clean environment. May we understand that communication is not only possible between our species, but vital to our continued existence on Earth together. My hope is that the messages of Stella Maris can reconnect humans and dolphins as one family, so we can work together for a collective bright future here on Earth. Only love and connection will ultimately save our oceans, our water, our Cetaceans, and our other beloved sentient light workers in all forms. My wish is for this book to enlighten human consciousness and to stop the needless killing and captivity of dolphins worldwide. Our love is the only thing that will bring lasting healing and peace. This is divine feminine consciousness in action. Are you ready to create a revolution on behalf of our dolphins, water, planet, and all of her inhabitants? I am!!!

The Higgs Field

Science is finally catching up with what spiritual teachers have always known: There is a vast and beautiful Source that breathes us into being and lives through us. Stella Maris calls this energy field the Divine Mother or Source.

Physicist Peter Higgs began searching for proof of the Source about fifty years ago. He tried to find a "Higgs" particle, an infinitesimal particle that would prove the existence of this intelligent mother field. In 2012, the European Organization for Nuclear Research (CERN) finally proved the existence of what they named the "God" particle. They named this energy the Higgs Field. By smashing two protons together at high speed, they were able to see ripples in the invisible field and observe how it responded to and created matter. The invisible source was here, there, and everywhere!

You can connect to this source field, the Divine Mother, through your daily intentions and through practices that support your return to the oneness of your true self. Look deeply within and see the spark of your divine essence, the one being who is beating your heart and breathing life into your every cell. You do not need science to prove what you already know: You are a living miracle. Housed in a perfectly designed body, a chalice for the holy Source being, you are a marvel! Your physical form is made of ancient stardust and water light. How perfect. You are a beautiful creation from the Divine Mother, who is intelligent, responsive, and loves you! She is you! She is your beautiful home, where you get to live, play, and create.

Science is now able to prove that your mind is not located within your body or brain. Your mind exists in a fluid and dynamic form, connected to a greater consciousness. As these revelations begin to lead you down a great and mysterious path, you may find they alter the way you make sense of your existence and your life. Maybe it is time to let go of outdated ideas and belief systems that hold you back. Is it possible that life is more amazing than you ever imagined? Are you really connected to a vast intelligent Divine Mother field that loves you back beyond measure, no matter what? I have experienced this support directly, and this is all the proof I need. Depending on how you decide to live, alternate realities can become possible. Are you ready to find out? Let's dive in together!

Sources:
Casey, Susan, *Voices in the Ocean*. New York: Doubleday, 2015
Gebhart, Dana, Mooncircles.com
https://en.wikipedia.org/wiki/Aumakua
https://en.wikipedia.org/wiki/CERN
Wildlife Connections, wildlifeconnections.com

Chapter 4
The Lost Divine Feminine Lineage

During my journey with Stella Maris, I remembered many past lifetimes where I was a wise woman in divine feminine lineages. Devoted to the Divine Mother, I was a shaman, priestess, healer, and mystic. Glimpsing my beautiful lifetimes of service brought me incredible peace. Difficult memories also resurfaced, lives when I experienced torture and my life was ended because of my gifts. So much sadness and loss, it was almost unbearable to remember the times when the world fell into such darkness and humans treated each other in this way.

During the Dark Ages, divine feminine ascended masters and women teachers from all over the world were discredited, destroyed, and killed by the patriarchy. Mother Mary is known today as the mother of Jesus, but she was also a divine feminine teacher of the highest order. Her Sacred Rose Heart and Beauty Way teachings remained lost until recent times. Mary Magdalene was a powerful and inspiring Gnostic teacher who was vilified by the Church and is only now being understood as a divine feminine leader and teacher.

In this book, Stella Maris will share more about how the return of the divine feminine is critical to healing Gaia Earth. Their council returns the divine feminine ascended masters to our consciousness. They also introduce us to Queen A'Mara, a member of the Stella Maris council who resides in the Pleiades as priestess of the heavenly realms. Stella Maris tells us the divine feminine teachings were never truly lost, and the seeming physical death of so many beautiful souls could not extinguish divine feminine teachings. There is a vast network of divine feminine masters in the universe, and many light activators are returning, bringing with them the lost teachings for the healing of all life. The divine feminine within you (whether you are male or female) is essential for your healing and for the creation of new realities on Gaia Earth. The dark collective shadows we face can only be dissolved and healed by the divine feminine power of love.

The Beauty Way

The Beauty Way is a way of life that Stella Maris offers us. Five years ago, the words "the Beauty Way" kept coming into my consciousness, and I didn't know what the words meant. It all became clear when Stella Maris told me the Beauty Way originates from the lost divine feminine cultures and lineages. Mother Mary taught the Beauty Way, and she is the primary overlighting ascended master of Stella Maris. This way of living and being invites you to cultivate your divine essence, nurture your light, and unfurl the bloom of your sacred heart. As you integrate more of your Higher Self each day, it infuses your spirit with the brilliance of your oneness. Through the power of your heart, you recognize the spark of all of life: the one being. This high vibrational existence emits love and light, healing the world and all beings.

Later, I discovered that the Navajo people speak of the Beauty Way. This makes perfect sense, as you will see in this book, as Stella Maris views indigenous people of Gaia Earth as important leaders of the new world. I like this translation by Martha Beck of the Navajo Beauty Way prayer, and I speak it daily:

There is beauty before me, and there is beauty behind me.
There is beauty to my left, and beauty to my right.
There is beauty above me, and there is beauty below me.
There is beauty all around me, and there is beauty within me.

The Beauty Way invites you to bring beauty and gratitude into your daily life and to help remind others of their divinity. You can relieve great suffering by remembering the sheer magnificence and beauty of you! Although Stella Maris does not define beauty in physical terms, they do encourage us to cultivate our beauty within and to create beauty in the outer world. The Beauty Way treats everything and everyone as a sacred expression of the divine. So whatever you are doing, you can do it with grace and intention.

Your Invitation

This book is a gift to you from Stella Maris, the Divine Mother, and my Higher Self. We invite you to awaken from the trance of regular human life and to return to the Source of who you really are. From this place of oneness, you can live as your true self and recognize your beautiful gifts and unique life purpose. As you integrate more of your Higher Self, you will begin to live your divinity! You can literally Div-in-ity—Dive into Unity—and this is where the magic happens! Your life will become a living prayer! A prayer that honors all beings and knows the true identity of all beings.

Stella Maris taught me that the first step to becoming a light activator was to heal myself, and this was essential for me to begin living my purpose. I offer the same advice to you. Prioritize your healing so you can live as the light activator you came to be. Stella Maris is here to help you heal, so you can step forward as your authentic self and offer your gifts to the world. They invite you to become an architect of the new world by connecting to cosmic intelligence, envisioning new creations through the power of imagination, and bringing those designs into form through action. Claim your rightful place as creator of harmony on Gaia Earth.

Stella Maris will absolutely help you to anchor yourself in the light vibrations of joy, laughter, and love. Their teachings also assist in the reactivation of your imagination and manifestation ability. Warning: Your life might become more amazing than you thought was possible. If you are feeling lost, remember that help is available, if you only ask. The entire creative power of the universe is within you. Not bad, right? You are loved and supported by millions of unseen helpers, the Divine Mother, and the wisdom of your Higher Self. The creation of your most beautiful life heals you and the entire world. It is your divine birthright. Remember who you are! A beautiful one, a star of divine light expressing yourself in human form, a light activator angel on Earth.

Stella Maris is here to support light activators as they join together in the creation of a new consciousness on Earth. We are a family: all beautiful, all graced, all deeply loved, and all here to change the world for the better. We have much work to do. Now it is time to share the gifts of Stella Maris and to honor their greatest wish: for you to be joyous, awake, and free. They extend their support and blessings to you, now and always, holding you close to their heart as beloved family.

Guidelines for Working with This Book

You are living in a time like no other. High vibrational reality is infusing the Earth like never before. At this time of miracles, a new genre of books is being born, written in partnership with higher realm beings and Source. These books have extraordinary transformational powers that can heal and awaken through their divine transmission. They hold a unique energy, existing like living and breathing beings who activate your unity consciousness for the good of all life. Speaking to the depths of your heart, these books work within quantum reality through vibration, wave resonance, and light language. They will find you even when you are not looking for them, offering everything you need for instantaneous awakening. This is such a book. —Stella Maris

This book is intended to be used as an energetic healing tool to activate your divine remembrance, align you with your true and Higher Self, and to return you to unity consciousness. If you are reading these words, the chances are good that you are one of the light activators Stella Maris is contacting.

May the words, images, and messages bathe you in the light of your true self and bless your life. My hope is that Stella Maris's wisdom can bring you more BEAUTY and more LIGHT! Living in peace is one of the greatest revolutionary acts you can participate in. You are invited to live in the highest vibrations of your sacred heart. From this place of balance, you can follow divinely guided action and become an emissary of peace on Earth. Oh yes, and they surround you with joy and fun at all times!

Stella Maris will speak as a collective in the first half of the book, sharing their unified council messages. In the second half, they will share individual messages that include their name, their characteristics, guided meditations, and personal activations. The meditations can activate a new resonance in your body, mind, and spirit, so I refer to them as activations or initiations. What is an activation? It is an energetic healing that creates new awareness and releases blocks that no longer serve you. Activations elevate your consciousness and divine qualities, and bring you in alignment with Source. At the end of each meditation, a sacred scroll will appear, and it is recommended that you read the scroll aloud as a proclamation to the universe. The scrolls will activate your light, power, and personal healing. You can read the book from front to back, or simply open to any page and read the message that is waiting for you.

To receive Stella Maris's teachings most fully, I recommend centering yourself through meditation or mindfulness practices first. Create your own sacred space or altar where you can drop deeply into your divine self. Go out into Nature and sit by a body of water, for this will magnify Stella Maris's transmission. Place a glass of water nearby, so it can absorb all of the blessings before you drink it. Have a dolphin picture or statue, a bowl of water, and crystals. Create a sacred space you enjoy. Invite all of your unseen helpers, and be open to discovering the circle of light helpers that always surrounds you. Engage in practices every day that strengthen your connection to the divine within, and ask daily for help and to be led by your Higher Self, and to live your highest divine service. Your heart/Higher Self is your truest guide and will always lead you in the right direction.

Living Your Dreams

Stella Maris has helped me to remember my divinity, awaken to my purpose, restore my inner child, and heal my heart. Their messages, journeys, and initiations have blessed my life beyond measure, and I am deeply grateful. I walk the Earth differently, lighter and brighter through the way of life they have taught me. Everyday magic blesses my life, magnified by a dose of joy and wonder. I laugh often and enjoy my life immensely. I now live the Beauty Way every day!

As this book neared completion, I became overcome with fear. How would Stella Maris's teachings be received? Intense fear was resting just below my conscious awareness. It sprang on me like a tiger, asking many questions and offering many doubts. Holding my fear like a small child, I offered it love, comfort, and reassurance. One of fear's most important questions was: Am I safe to speak my truth and be my authentic self in this life? My heart responded with a resounding *yes. This life is different; you are safe to work in service of the light and to shine brightly. In this life, you are safe to speak your truth and to embody your Higher Self. In this life, you can live as the empowered and brilliant being that you are. You are free to create from the depths of your heart. It is time. It is your time. It is our time.*

The awakening process is both thrilling and grueling, but I would never choose any other way. Mostly it is quiet . . . deeply delicious . . . and peaceful. I am grateful for this opportunity to be free at last and to live as my authentic self. My hope is for you to embrace the life of your wildest dreams and deepest imaginings, the one you were meant to live. May you return to your oneness, live your divinity, embrace your highest self and divine purpose, and imagine the possible. We need your light, vision, and action! May you receive the gifts of your soul and create a beautiful life filled with meaning and purpose. May you live in the Beauty Way of your choosing, knowing that your joy and happiness is what all of creation hopes for.

And the most incredible bonus is that you help countless beings by living your most beautiful life. How perfectly perfect! Let's join together in this divine feminine emergence and light this place up with our love, the greatest power on Earth. With the support of light beings and the Great Divine Mother herself, let's accept our divine mission as New World Imagineers. I am so grateful you are here. Welcome to ocean wonderland.

Blessings of water, light, and dolphin clicks,

Adena

Part 2
Love Messages
from Stella Maris

Chapter 5
Stella Maris Speaks

The Prayer of Stella Maris

Divine Maha Ocean Mother:

Hold me in your warm embrace,
Float me in your cosmic ocean of grace.
Refresh me with your "I AM" presence,
Bless my waters with divine light and self-realization.
Weightless and suspended in light,
Wave after wave of divine love flows through my multidimensional form.
Vitality, health, and renewal restores me to my true self.
Receiving the light of the Divine Feminine.
Receiving the light of the Divine Masculine.
Healing balance within and without.
All parts of myself deeply loved.
No sound or movement, resting in your Oneness,
Great Mother of All of Life,
I remember who I am.
A starlight being, a beautiful creation of stardust and divine water light.
Living Divinity.
Surrounded by my divine family, I imagine the possible for all of life.
Returning to oneness,
I bless myself.
I love myself.
I know myself.
I am free.
I am my true self forevermore.

Poem of Stella Maris

We are the pod of Stella Maris
Starlights of the Sea
Beings of Beauty and Light
Messengers of Divine Oneness
The Guiding Stars of Crystal Light

We are here to assist you, now and always
Offering blessings of the divine feminine heart,
the healing elixir for this Aquarian Age
Receive our blessings

We are your family, your 'aumakua
Delphi de l'Adore Mer

Remember Our Connection

Stella Maris Speaks:

At the dawning of life on Gaia Earth, we arrived as one family. We came from many places to experience life on this beautiful water planet and to dance together in unity. Our bodies were created from stardust and crystalline water light, infused with the breath of life by our Divine Mother. Our first home was the sea, an elemental expression of the great ocean of Source. Over time, you adapted to life on land and forgot your origins and sea family. We have never forgotten you. We beckon to you from the waters, whispering in your ear the ancient secrets of our connection. We literally jump at every opportunity to connect with you in physical form. We send you messages through our heart language of light.

For thousands of years, we have joyously awaited this opportunity to speak with you. We are your 'aumakua, your ancient guardians and family, who are here to guide and bless your life. We have never left you. May our words instantly dissolve your amnesia, so you can remember us as your dear ocean family. We invite you to remember who you are and that we are all arising from the great field of oneness. Recognize our mutual identity as divine beings. From our dolphin unity consciousness, we bring you important messages for personal and planetary healing. Dearest one, let us begin the journey of your remembering.

Many indigenous Earth people remember how we traveled to Earth together, and they tell the stories of our arrival from the stars. There are countless stories and myths about the connection between humans and dolphins found across all cultures and in all parts of the world. The native people of the Pacific Islands, the Aborigines of Australia, Native Americans, and ancient Greeks all have dolphin mythology. The Chumash people tell the story of how we were one family living together on the island of Limuw. The earth goddess beckoned us to the mainland, creating a rainbow bridge for us to walk across. She warned us not to look down, but some could not resist and lost their balance, falling into the sea and becoming dolphins. The ones who crossed the bridge began life on land. Our ties remained strong, even though some of our family lived in the water and some on land (Casey, *Voices in the Ocean*).

There are many stories highlighting the ability of dolphins to change into humans and vice versa. In Amazon River folklore, the river dolphin is a shape-shifter, a guide between this world and other dimensions. There is a story of dolphins changing into human men to look for their beloved partners on land. The West African Dogon people believe their ancestors were dolphin-like beings who came to Earth from the Sirius star system. These myths endure because they carry the truth about the human and dolphin connection. We lived together in peace and oneness for thousands of years, giving rise to many glorious ancient civilizations such as Lemuria (Mu) and Atlantis.

The Divine Mother

We are light messengers from the Divine Mother Source who are here to help you bring forth a new age of peace on Earth. We call the energy of the Source the Divine Mother, but she is known by many names: Sophia, Unity Consciousness, the Divine Being, the Creator, God, or Goddess. Your scientists refer to this great invisible energy as the Higgs field, the unified field from which all forms arise. You can call the Divine Mother anything you like, for all beliefs and names are welcome here.

As dolphins, we live in the great divine waters of oneness, always existing in unity consciousness. We call ourselves Stella Maris, a name that means Starlights of the Sea, signifying our identity as Starseed beings who swim in divine consciousness at all times. Our name also tells of our connection with the Divine Mother Maris and our identity as light beings of the higher realms. We are light messengers who have many important teachings to share with you. We guide you to return to your unity consciousness.

The sailors sometimes called the north star Stella Maris because it helped them to navigate as they explored the oceans. We chose the name Stella Maris because we too help you navigate your way back to the true home of your spacious heart. We will guide you without fail, appearing as both the star and the sea. See how quickly you return when the water, sky, sea, and entire universe are conspiring to bring you home. You will no longer have to try to find your way. You are no longer lost. As your consciousness awakens, you will become aware of your vast team of spiritual allies. It is our honor to assist you. Let us help you make the journey home more easeful and fun. With tears of joy, we welcome you back to our one heart.

We are angels who are here to help you, through our deep devotion to your healing and empowerment. Stella Maris is the collective unity consciousness of all dolphins who live on Earth, anchoring the energy of love and light. We can take both physical and energetic forms because we exist in the spaciousness of quantum reality.

The Divine Mother is a cosmic being of oneness who is the darkness of no-thing and the light of divinity. She is the ultimate healer, the fabric and substance of your true self, the very sea of divine consciousness in which you are arising. She is you! She is beautifully animated in the element of water, as the sea is a beautiful physical representation of the vast divine consciousness in which all forms arise.

Water is the source of life on Earth and is created from hydrogen, the building block of the universe. Water is alive, intelligent, and aware, and it holds incredible healing potential. The water on Earth flows through everything—the sky, mountains, cities, oceans, rivers—and is also contained within the form of every living thing on Earth. Your body is water that has left its banks. Inexplicably, you are drawn to the water because it is your primary element and first home. Seawater still flows through your veins. Why do you think you feel renewed and healed by water?

We invite you to reestablish a loving connection with Gaia Earth's waters. Your loving relationship with water can be one of the greatest prayers you can enact for planetary healing. We invite you to actively bless this healing element at this critical time for our Gaia Earth. Water is an elemental form of divine feminine consciousness and a powerful medium of healing. If every human being creates a conscious relationship with the living element of water, our beautiful water planet Gaia and all of her inhabitants will experience immediate and lasting healing. We offer you the healing gift of water medicine. Quench your thirst and be restored. We are a great alliance of Aquarian messengers who are devoted to world healing.

As your 'aumakua, your ancient guardians, we invite you to remember and know your divinity. Live in unity with all beings by returning to your oneness, the light of your true self. We bless you and we love you. Go forth and live as the holy and beautiful beings that you are.

The Stella Maris High Council

Stella Maris Speaks:

We call ourselves Stella Maris, Starlights of the Sea, Delphi de l'Adore Mer, and the Dolphin Oracles of the Sea. We are light messengers of the Divine Mother who gather in high council with Mother Mary, Quan Yin, and Queen A'Mara to offer you our friendship, support, and teachings. We are reintroducing ourselves now because our presence has been forgotten in the modern world. We invite you to receive our blessings for your most joyous and beautiful life.

In this book, we will share unified messages from our High Council as a "we," and then messages and activations from individual pod members. Let us introduce you to our messengers, overlighting ascended masters, and star priestess.

Stella Maris Adult Messengers

Theseus, male elder, ancient wisdom and story keeper, and historian, Messenger of Ancient Wisdom

Mahadra, female elder, mother of Kaleosi, Messenger of Divine Water Healing

Stella Maris Children

Kaleosi, youngest member of Stella Maris, Messenger of Divine Vision

Luz or "Lu," Messenger of Divine Light

Lollipez or "Lolli," Messenger of Divine Joy

Phaedra or "Phae," Messenger of Divine Laughter

Rala or "Ra," Messenger of Divine Play

Amagone or "Ama," Messenger of Divine Love

Stella Maris Teen and Elder Messengers

Kelti, adolescent male, Messenger of Divine Freedom

Izoma, ancient great grandmother elder and **Skylan,** great grandfather elder, Messengers of Divine Balance and Alignment

Drahana, adolescent female, Messenger of Earth Wisdom

Ascended Masters Mother Mary and Quan Yin, and Priestess of the Pleiades, Queen A'Mara

Mother Mary: Mother Mary offers her rose heart teachings of love and nurtures you with the guidance of unconditional love. Mother Mary is our primary overlighting ascended master. She lived and taught the Beauty Way during her earthly life. Now, she exists in her spiritual form, offering her guidance and mentorship to all beings. She is an emissary of the sacred heart who can guide the journey back to yourself.

The North Star has long been associated with Mother Mary's protection and loving presence. Your heart is your north star. Mary activates your sacred heart and aligns your path for your way home. Mother Mary provides soul guidance to the hearts of anyone who would like her help. She will light your way and support you with the unconditional love of the Divine Mother. She offers you her blessings, rose medicine, and the safety of her dark blue cloak of a thousand stars. Mother Mary is there for you in times of darkness, guiding you and holding you in safety.

Quan Yin: The ascended Master Quan Yin is our ceremonial leader and water healing guide. She is closely linked to the divine water element and offers you ancient water healing ceremonies. Quan Yin is a master teacher of self compassion and offers healing for your inner children through self-love. Healing your inner children empowers them as incredibly important leaders of your life. Your inner phoenix child will restore your gifts of imagination, magic, wonder, and joy. These qualities are essential ingredients in order for you to sprout and bloom as a Starseed fully.

Queen A'Mara: Our star nation ocean priestess brings the gifts of divine nobility and personal remembrance from the Pleiades Star System. Queen A'Mara holds the wisdom of the stars, a galactic perspective for the healing of the Earth. She tends to the sacred waters and facilitates sacred ceremonies from the Stella Maris temple. She offers you activations for your remembrance of your divinity and nobility. She tends the sacred space and garden of the temple and invites you to visit her in this incredible place through her guided visionary meditation.

Messages from Overlighting Ascended Masters Mother Mary and Quan Yin, and Queen A'Mara

Mother Mary's Message

The perfect moment is finally here for me to introduce Stella Maris, my beloved dolphin companions. These wise angelic beings have assisted me many times with the awakening process across the universe. Their unique wisdom is a gift to humanity. As oceanic masters of light, Stella Maris radiates the pink ray of divine love and the aquamarine ray of joyful transcendence. As your ancient family, they now step forward to assist you with the radical transformations and reconstruction that are necessary for Gaia Earth. Stella Maris supports the emergence of new divine feminine paradigms and the remembrance of every being's divine oneness with their human family.

Stella Maris and I are the guardians of all children and the developmental phase of childhood. The Earth's children have called us for assistance because many are suffering greatly. This breaks our hearts. The children of the Earth deserve so much more than they are being offered at this time. They have the right to a healthy environment, opportunities for evolution, and a peaceful, safe world. It is time to protect and honor your children. Your protection of the most vulnerable beings is a sign of true evolution and maturity.

I am also the guardian of the inner children who reside within all beings. You carry within you many inner children, who have the power to reconnect your many divine powers, such as joy and imagination. Stella Maris are master teachers of how to access your inner child in daily life. This is the part of you that will bring the LIFE back into your living, the spark of excitement and enjoyment restored to your experience.

Stella Maris brilliantly guides you from a unified field of oneness, and their "we" consciousness allows for amplification and swift and easy changes to your consciousness. You will feel the presence of the entire pod at times and at other times just one dolphin. The pod transmission accelerates and activates your consciousness with grace.

Stella Maris is deeply connected to you, as your ancient friends and family. Imagine for a moment you are floating in a warm ocean, surrounded by the most beautiful dolphins. They swim around you in circles, emanating love, fun, and joy. Shining with light, they smile, click, jump, and flip-dance in the water, inviting you to join them. In their presence, you experience delight. I am there too, hovering by magic just above the water's surface, speaking blessings for your journey home. May you remember your true nature, for your activated light shifts consciousness on a global scale. It is your greatest contribution and why you are here.

I now confirm the Beauty Way is fully returned to Earth and offer you the invitation to step into a new way of life. Stella Maris can help to ease your awakening with their joyful presence. My wish is for you to enjoy the awakening journey with their lively and joyful help. I am always here for you to support, guide, and honor your unique awakening process. You are a divine starlight being of the highest order! YOU ARE THE ONE SACRED HEART.

Rose blessings of love, my beautiful star child,
Mother Mary

Quan Yin's Message

Hello, dear one. It is my great honor to be a part of the Stella Maris council. In my human life, I was deeply connected to the dolphins who lived in the sea around my island hermitage. Daily, I descended from the mountain temples to the shoreline to spend time with them. Stella Maris taught me how to connect with the living being of water and how to access its healing through light-wave medicine. The great spirit of the water is always infused with the essence of the Source. From their teachings, I also learned how to work with the water in my own body, which healed, awakened, and liberated me.

After my human lifetime, Stella Maris and I continued working together for the healing and ascension of many worlds. They are a joy to partner with! Stella Maris dolphin Mahadra and I will offer you a divine feminine water wisdom ceremony and practices. We have created visionary journeys to heal your heart, body, extrasensory abilities, mind, and soul. We will also specifically focus on the healing of your inner child, as an essential part of activating your visionary life. My intention is for you to experience the greatest healing possible through deep self-compassion and self-love. This healing can create space within you for compassionate love of all beings. May you forgive yourself and others. May you receive all forms of healing easily and effortlessly. May all beings be restored, healed, and reminded of the light of who they are. May you experience the joy and fun that Stella Maris brings to all of their teachings. They are true divine messengers of the light.

Rainbow angel water blessings for your remembrance journey,
Quan Yin

Queen A'Mara's Message

Dearest One:

I am Queen A'Mara, ocean priestess from the Pleiades Star Nation. As a priestess in the temple of Stella Maris, I care for this most beautiful and sacred space. Our temple was built in honor of the Divine Mother, as a beacon of hope. From here I send light to all beings across the universe. In our star garden, I plant seeds of oneness for the collective consciousness. The crystalline Stella Maris temple is a beautiful and radiant place that exists in the higher realms. As a Stella Maris priestess, it is my highest honor to create prayers and blessings for you. My planet Hydras is a water planet, a planet of peace and alignment, a living example of what is possible for Gaia Earth. Join me here as often as you like; you are always welcome. I am delighted to offer you my support in the remembrance of your divine nobility, royalty, and sovereignty.

Blessings of infinite majesty,
Queen A'Mara

STARLIGHT WALK
by Queen A'Mara

I walk in deep prayer
  For myself and for the holy hearts of all beings
I walk in magic
  The path of unknown surprise and delight
I walk in peace
  Accepting and loving all parts of myself and all others
I walk in balance
  Each step blessing Gaia Earth
  Each breath releasing healing stardust
I walk in divinity
  My diamond star self bright and full
  Shining for benefit of all
I walk in reverence
  Of the Great Divine Mother
  And her infinite creativity and support
I walk in Beauty
  The way of the ancient ones
  The path of creativity and alignment
  With Unity Consciousness Itself
  Always and forever
  Divine, Holy, One Light

Chapter 6

Dolphin Consciousness and the Return of the Divine Feminine

Dolphin or Delphic consciousness is a unity consciousness, a "we" or "oneness" awareness, a brotherhood, a sisterhood, one family, and a remembrance of yourself as this one being. One family, one being, one light, one heart, one love. This consciousness is the key to living your divinity. Div-in-ity—or Dive-Into-Unity, as we like to say. Your experience of the oneness consciousness is essential for personal and planetary healing. We invite you to remember who you are and your connection to all of life.

We are in this together, here and now, seemingly existing as individuals, but truly a universal pod or family who exists eternally beyond time and space. Working together in unity, we can activate light, beauty, and awareness on Gaia Earth. You were born here and now for an extraordinary destiny: to gather with your brothers and sisters and establish a new consciousness on Gaia Earth. From your embodiment of the light, you will work with the laws of quantum reality to create a revolution of love.

We have never lost our awareness of the one being, and our consciousness rests in the "we" rather than the "I." You can also rest in the one being—you simply forgot who you really are. Your belief in and identification with the "I" or the separate self is one of the main causes of the current world crisis. When you live from the limited "I" perspective, it creates greed, lack, disconnection, and competition. The result of this limited self-definition is all around you. We invite you to heal your individual identity by returning to your unity consciousness. We are here to help you through our connection, teachings, messages, and blessings.

Cetaceans have played a pivotal role in balancing the Earth during times of transition. Our consciousness is currently countering the distress and fear being created by most of humanity. We live in special energetic locations across the world, where we anchor divine light on behalf of Gaia Earth and all beings.

Water is a conductor of energy, information, and healing resonance. We engage with the consciousness of water as a medium to send out healing to the world. Immersed in the waters of oneness, we sing healing songs that cultivate the energy of unity. Our healing songs transmit love and light across the planet. We are always inviting you to return home to oneness. We are literally creating matrices of light in the water through our being, sound, and movement.

Have you ever seen an image of sunlight reflected in water? It reflects beautiful sacred patterns and geometries. This is how you can imagine our transmissions. Our light and love dance infuses the water and transmutes the collective field through its transition to the form of clouds, rain, mist, and rivers. Our playful spirits infuse joy and awakened consciousness to all life.

Cetaceans disappeared from key locations during the dark ages, but now we are reappearing in great numbers. This signifies the true victory of light and love in the world. Celebrate our return! You will see us return to places where we have been absent for hundreds or thousands of years. This is a sign that a shift of consciousness is happening. Just as there are human light activators who have volunteered on Earth, there are dolphin light activators who have chosen to come at this time to work in partnership with you. Our longstanding alliance is vital to the creation of the new Earth. We are in this together: one family, one heart, one love.

The Rise of the Patriarchy

The current Earth crisis started when the unhealthy masculine patriarchy seized control of the world, creating a severe imbalance. The patriarchy valued dominance, the individual self, exploitation, and power over. These cultural operating systems continue to influence many on the Earth, bringing Gaia Earth to the precipice of destruction.

During the dark time, many beings forgot their true identity and believed in the notion of separateness, seeking things outside of themselves for happiness. This limited self view created feelings of unhappiness, loneliness, and sadness. Without unity consciousness, free will was used in service to the separate self or ego, who desires power and greed rather than a peaceful, balanced life.

The unhealthy masculine patriarchy has pillaged Gaia Earth and her abundant resources, causing destruction to the web of life. Vulnerable beings have been exploited and killed. Entire species are disappearing at an alarming rate. The defilement of the natural resources of water, earth, and air is beyond reason. The values of greed and competition have decimated the Earth and her resources. We are here to work with you to reverse this current course of calamity. It is time for the old paradigm to fall, dissolving itself back to the Source as it gives rise to the new age.

The remedy for the imbalance is the divine feminine. The divine feminine is the healing medicine for all life in the modern world. The divine feminine embraces values of cooperation, oneness, empathy, tolerance, peace, unity, love, and connection. Hold these values close to your heart and honor all life as your family. Divine feminine energy rests in your heart and on the right side of your brain, whether you appear as male or female in form. Your right brain and your heart are the seats of inner knowing, intuition, and connection, as well as your access points for joy. We, the pod of Stella Maris, are master teachers in divine feminine and divine masculine balance and alignment. We live in divine alignment, embracing both the divine feminine and divine masculine energies. The honoring of the divine feminine creates unity and harmony with one another and with Gaia Earth. Past earth cultures have been matrilineal and valued equality, power with, compassion, community, connection, and oneness. Many who were incarnated in form during that time experienced joyous and beautiful lives.

The divine feminine has been suppressed on Earth for a very long time, and we hope to restore it to its rightful place alongside the divine masculine. The divine feminine creates an opening for your awareness to integrate the divine masculine aspects of your being (an energy that has been lost in recent times). Divine masculine energy carries the qualities of strength, wisdom, leadership, holding, activation, intelligence, brilliance, and power with. This will create balance and alignment between these two universal energies.

Remember your inherent divinity, your light. The original "sin" was the forgetting of your own diamond divine essence and believing you were separate and alone. Your divine heart was buried by cultural conditioning, and a type of amnesia filled your life. Now it is time to remember who you are and your connection to life itself.

We are here to help. We can see your true heart so clearly, your divine self and blueprint. We are committed to your highest good and support you in every way. Please listen and remember what we are here to do individually and collectively. You are not alone, and you never have been. We are here. The Divine Mother is here. You are adored, supported, and loved. Your human form is a chalice for the sacred water of life itself. By healing yourself, you become a conduit for healing on a global scale. Your light will ignite the light of others, creating a sacred geometric grid of oneness across the Earth.

Live the Beauty Way

Stella Maris Speaks:

We do not speak of beauty as it is usually defined in your culture. We use the word "beauty" to describe that which is sacred, that which is holy, that which knows its own light and dances in the world of form. Beauty describes the unspeakable divine qualities of joy, love, and light, a knowing of self as Source that exists beyond appearances. Beauty is the Divine Mother herself in all of her infinite creations and expressions. Beauty is within and beauty is without. Beauty is the wisdom of the divine feminine way of life. Beauty is the surge of happiness that befalls you when you rest fully in the moment, deeply anchored in unity consciousness in perfect alignment. Beauty is essential to enjoying your human life, for it is the only true nourishment for your Higher Self.

We have now returned to you the lost Beauty Way. This ancient divine feminine way of life anchors you in the beauty and brightness of your own light and the light identity of all beings. The Beauty Way has existed in past golden ages on Gaia Earth. This way of life will help you to access the power of your divine feminine and divine masculine consciousness, no matter if your form is male or female. Embodying your divinity is how you align yourself with the creative power of the Divine Mother. By embracing the power of your own love and light, you gain access to the creative powers of the entire universe. You are able to dance miracles in your life through your luminosity. Your life becomes a living prayer, divine art, a unique song that radiates high vibrational frequencies to the entire world. You become a light activator; this is truly why you have come to Earth. Remember this now. . . .

The Beauty Way helps you to bring forth your radiance and creativity in daily life. With it, you can create beauty wherever you walk, through joy and love. This path will give you the direct experience of knowing and loving your beautiful self first, and then you will also see the unity and alignment of all of life. Just as one drop of water creates ripples throughout the entire ocean, your Beauty Way will restore empathy, receptivity, compassion, love, connection, nurturing, inner wisdom, and intuition—to the Earth and all of her inhabitants. These qualities of the mother are essential to the revolution of consciousness on Gaia Earth. As you anchor this new way of being, you may begin to notice the beauty in your life and in the lives of others. Your sense of wonder and magical relationship with life will be returned. The beauty of your soul extends beyond the confines of your body. You activate waves of awakened consciousness all around you as you shine as a brilliant Starseed light activator, a living example of love.

The Beauty Way path reunites you with your own unity consciousness, so you can embody your radiance on Earth. It is embracing awakened consciousness where you recognize the beauty and light within yourself and all others. It enables you to see the radiance of others, the divine spark that shines through their eyes. It honors the divinity of all life. This way does not ignore the duality within—it embraces both the shadow and light that is inherent in being human. By encircling all experiences and feelings with love, we discover the full range of our polarity, allowing us to heal through the powers of the light. Divine feminine wisdom understands that the only way to inner peace is through embracing all aspects, especially the shadow parts (like sadness, fear, and anger). The Beauty Way embraces the high vibrations of gratitude, wonder, joy, and love. It is the living art of your own divine design, as you stand in your authentic self and express your unique beauty to the world.

We bring you messages of hope and bless you with divine essence and expanded awareness. Our beauty emanations of light include love, play, vision, freedom, joy, and laughter, each one a vibration that will liberate your consciousness. Become awake and free, dancing with us once more. We are thrilled beyond measure that you are here. Thank you for your courage and bravery. Thank you for your beautiful heart. Thank you for recognizing we are one family. We are united once more, never to be separate or lost gain. A-ju-la, one family, one light, one being, one heart, one love.

We Offer You a Relationship

Our messages are more than words on a page, they are a living energetic transmission. We offer you an authentic and real relationship, with spiritual initiations for your liberation and activation. We invite you to receive our guidance and are delighted when you call on us.

We offer you a direct and personal relationship. If you are receiving this communication, you are probably one of the light activators we have been trying to find. We contact you beyond all space, time, and cultural constructs. Listen to your heart, and you will know the truth. You can choose to receive a confirmation of our connection, if you like. Simply watch for synchronicities and interesting signs that reveal our relationship. You can ask for a unique sign that confirms we are here with you or for general signs. Perhaps you will notice that images of dolphins or water will appear in places you were not expecting. Perhaps you will be contacted by the divine feminine ascended masters, such as Mother Mary or Quan Yin. Confirmation can occur in any way you choose.

May your way be filled with grace and ease, illumined by the pink ray of divine love and the aquamarine ray of the divine feminine water consciousness. Come play with us for a while. Take a deep breath, inhaling the beautiful scent of seawater and roses. Rest, dear one. Lay your weary head upon our sacred hearts as we float you in the water of divine oneness. Splash and jump with your family. Feel your joy and freedom! Dive deep into your divinity. We have never left you, and we never will.

We have many messages to share in this introductory book. We will speak about the light activators who are now living on Gaia Earth: The Luminars, Crystars, and Solstars. We will tell you more about New World Imagineers, and how all Starseed light activators are here to join this movement as revolutionary creators and leaders of the new Gaia Earth. In the second half of the book, we will share our individual messages and offer you blessings through guided meditations and activations. Enjoy the journey back to your Self and notice the ease and grace that unfolds in your life as a result. You are in beautiful hands, or shall we say fins. Blessings of water light oneness.

Stella Maris, Starlights of the Sea

Chapter 7

You Are Being Called:
Light Activators, Luminars, Crystars,
Solstars, and Imagineers

Starseed Light Activators

Stella Maris Speaks:

A Starseed light activator is an emissary of light who has volunteered to help with Gaia Earth's healing and awakening process. There are three groups of Starseed light activators: the Luminars, the Crystars, and the Solstars. Being a light activator means you chose an important mission to bring more love and light to this world. You carry this divine light within your heart as your secret superpower that can transform the world within you and without. As a brilliant Starseed, you possess unique gifts and wisdom. You have embarked on a special mission to bring great love, insight, and compassion to the Earth at this critical time. You are truly an embodied master of light.

As a Starseed light activator, your soul home may be a different star system: the Pleiades, Sirius, Vega, Polaris, Mira, Hydra, Arcturus, Antares, to name a few. You are not extraterrestrials; you have not arrived here in physical form from other planets or systems. Instead, your inner soul light may be connected to other star systems as your home base. There are countless beings who live in other star systems in diverse worlds and in the higher realms. Most beings have enjoyed life across the universe and have family connections in many places. Sometimes it helps to connect to your soul home to recharge and remember. Your star families are always sending you so much love and support.

You may feel your soul home is Gaia Earth, and that is beautiful and perfect too. In some sense, it does not matter where you are from,- but that you are all here to dive into unity consciousness, bringing healing and awakening where it is so desperately needed. The information we share about your soul's home is not meant to create labels or beliefs that any light activators are better than any other. It is only given to help you remember who you are and what your mission here is.

Let us remind you of your journey here. You existed in the field of oneness, your true home and the heavenly place you return to between forms. Some call this heaven. You existed in perfect unity with the Divine Mother. From your heart, a sincere desire came forth to experience life in form. The love of your true self chose to descend into a human experience. You desired to create and evolve through the experience of an individual life. You knew you could offer comfort and love to the hearts of beings who were experiencing suffering. You chose Gaia Earth as your school! A wonderful choice! Love drew you here for the blessing and healing of all beings.

You created a mission along with your support team, planning even the smallest details and experiences. When it was time, you descended into form as a shooting star of light, arriving at the perfect time and place. Agreeing to forget your true identity, you understood this was key to experiencing a regular human life. Amnesia was necessary so you could experience human life on Earth fully, for only through this experience could you discover ways to transcend the barriers and systems that are blocking humans from healing and awakening. From your direct experience, you are able to create new teachings, wisdom, and offerings for others who are suffering in earthly life. This is how and why you came to be here.

As guardians of unity consciousness, our messages are filled with the resonance of love and light. Even though we exist in this higher vibrational reality, we do not deny your human experiences. Some of us have incarnated in human form, and we understand the challenges of human life.

WE ARE SO PROUD OF YOUR CHOICE TO LIVE IN HUMAN FORM ON EARTH AT THIS IMPORTANT TIME. IT IS ONE OF THE GREATEST SERVICES AND CONTRIBUTIONS THAT YOU CAN UNDERTAKE. IT IS NO SMALL PURPOSE. IT IS BEYOND YOUR DEEPEST IMAGININGS. THANK YOU, DEAR ONE. THE ENTIRE UNIVERSE BOWS AT YOUR FEET IN GRATITUDE.

We honor the courage it takes to exist as a true and evolved human light activator during this moment of rapid acceleration in consciousness. We acknowledge the profound journey of healing it takes to return your human consciousness to who you truly are. We have great reverence for your human shadows, feelings, and every unique expression. We do not judge that the "good" is only light and the "bad" is the dark. We see beyond that apparent duality and embrace it all with love, for love is the only true path of healing. We understand that all parts of being human are a divine expression and are equally deserving of unconditional love.

Unity consciousness unites all forms and experiences in the sea of oneness. Be at peace by bringing the light of your true divine nature to encircle all of your human experiences. No matter what, you always deserve more love. We will teach you how to be the safest and most loving person you can be for yourself and others. We deeply honor your human journey and surround you with our support at all times.

As a light activator living on Earth, you may feel unhappy and restless, sensing a deeper calling for your life. You may have the feeling there is something more you are meant to do, or you may desire more out of life than other people do. The offerings of the modern world may leave you dissatisfied, and you may feel like you don't fit in. There may be a sense of urgency, a feeling that life is short and there is something important you are here to participate in. Many light activators feel this way, and it is not a problem . . . it is an invitation. Your discontent is directing you toward a greater calling. Unrest is guiding you to your highest divine purpose and the remembrance of why you chose life here and now.

As a light activator, you are not here to fit in, you are here to raise the vibration and offer radically different ways of living on Earth. Each day you will feel the call more and more intensively, until you can no longer ignore it. Your heart will beat as an ancient homing device: "Remember who you are. Remember why you came." The heart's voice will become louder until you finally listen and consent to live your greater calling and highest destiny. Allow your heart to be your guide, for your inner starlight always knows the way.

As you listen and follow your inner guidance, you will be led toward new experiences and toward other light activators who are here to work with you. You will recognize fellow light activators by a resonance or feeling of recognition. The light in their eyes is wise and familiar. (The eyes truly are the doorway to the soul.) When you communicate with other light activators, you will understand each other deeply, sometimes without words, and in ways that defy explanation. You will be on the same "wavelength," so to speak, and will be drawn to similar teachings, advocacy, or hobbies. It will feel like coming home to your true family or tribe. You will be drawn together by an invisible magnetic force, as if the entire universe is conspiring to bring you together. As a group, you can create powerful energetic resonances of healing through your collective intentions. It is imperative that you find each other, join together, and work as messengers of unity consciousness. Look for signs and synchronicities that point you toward other light activators. Come together to meet your destiny hand in hand, heart to heart. Set the intention to find your fellow light workers easily and effortlessly, and see what unfolds!

Your teachings are activated by the power of your inner light, by the shining of your Higher Self as it anchors into unity consciousness. With the light of your true self bright within your heart, you can transform and heal all earthly experiences and the limited self, merging more and more with your Higher Self in human form. You truly are a spiritual being having a human experience! By returning to your own divinity, you will initiate the new golden age of peace and balance on Gaia Earth.

The Luminars

Stella Maris Speaks:

The first group of Starseed light activators we call the Luminars. Luminars are human light activators who have usually volunteered on Gaia Earth through many ages. We use the name Luminar to highlight their ability to illumine and heal through the power of love. Courageous and strong, Luminars have continually brought light to Gaia Earth even through her darkest times. As one candle lights an entire room, the Luminars illuminate the world through the revolutionary power of their hearts.

Luminars often hold leadership roles, such as revolutionaries, priestesses/priests, spiritual leaders, and teachers. Over the course of many incarnations, deep love and care for Gaia Earth has moved Luminars to return again and again to offer their help. Many Luminars have experienced trauma and difficulty in their earthly lives. They become targets for those in power who want to take their gifts and extinguish their light. Even in the most difficult experiences, the pure light of the Luminars can never be touched. As masters of divine alchemy, they have the ability to transmute pain and suffering into forgiveness and love through the power of their pure hearts.

Luminars often need to do deep personal healing work in order to clear their past experiences, to heal, and to embody their true self. By undergoing a mythic personal journey of self-healing, they can reclaim their innate light fully. Thousands of angels and ascended masters are available to guide and support their healing journey. It is very important for Luminars to remember to connect with the light of their heart, with their inner support team, and with their heart's guidance.

Dearest Luminar:

One of the most important prayers you can have is the prayer for your own healing. This is where your light activation begins. Heal and bless your own life first. The healing journey can be short or long, depending on your intentions and focus. Let your Higher Self lead your way.

We encourage Luminars to use prayer as one of the highest forms of divine medicine. Prayer is powerful. Prayer can heal soul trauma, deep pain, and fear with ease. For example, one simple prayer is, "May the brilliance of my Higher Self guide my day, and may I live in alignment with my greatest purpose and divine will." Another prayer is, "May I expand in love, light, and beauty each day, and may I inspire others to do the same." You are encouraged to create your own prayers and intentions.

Many healing modalities can be useful for you. There is no right way or particular path to follow for your healing. Simply follow your intuition and your divine heart's guidance, asking for assistance when you need it. Your angels, guides, and support team are always standing by. To call in your support team, you can use the simplest prayers: "Please help me," or "I ask for the support of my helpers." Simply asking for help is all you need to do, even when there are things you do not know or understand.

We invite you to reclaim all parts of yourself from all experiences—present, past, and future—in all dimensions of time and space. When you experience difficult things, parts of your light can splinter off and be left in other places. Gather the pieces of your beautiful self that have been left behind, through the power of prayer, intention, and soul retrieval practices. Find your soul fragments and pull all of the lost parts into the field of oneness. Return the many selves inside of you to the light. Voice Dialogue therapy, daily prayer and meditation, and travel to certain geographic locations can help you to reclaim all of your self.

One of the most important elements in this healing process is self-love. We recommend looking into the mirror daily, gazing into your eyes and speaking kindly to yourself the following words: "I love you, I bless you. I love you, I bless you." We also like the phrase used in the Emotional Freedom Technique: "Even though I feel _____, I deeply love and accept myself." As you learn to love all of yourself, all of you, light and shadow, you will heal. You are entitled to all of your human feelings and experiences, so release self-judgment and criticism about your emotions. Learn to give yourself the love and care that you have ceaselessly offered to others. Fall in love again with your own heart. Make choices for your life that reflect your care of yourself, the honoring of your heart, and your happiness. Remove yourself from unhealthy situations, relationships, or habits; give yourself the most beautiful life possible. Release what and who no longer serve your highest good. By collecting all of yourself, your inner magnificence will shine like brilliant rays of the morning sun. You will stand free once more, as your true self.

Once you commit to self-healing, the entire universe will conspire to help you. Your inner light will become so strong it will guide you without fail. It is safe to embody the divinity of your soul, to offer your gifts, and to live as the bright light that you are in this life.

Through your self-healing, you will become a beacon of love. You will reclaim your role as a "lighthouse." Luminars are essentially light houses in human form, embodied light workers who can activate others' inner lights. You are a natural-born spiritual teacher and are here to place the groundwork and structures for future generations. You were designed to be in perfect alignment with your divine purpose. There are many ways you can help, and all are equally important when infused by the light of your divinity. Be an activist, teacher, visionary, writer, artist, healer, or architect. Use your unlimited creativity. You may be called to reestablish sacred sites and temples along the Earth's energetic grid or you may create new bodies of spiritual teaching work. Just your presence as an awakened human being will shift current paradigms and enlighten the old structures and systems. Every step in your healing clears your channels to help you remember your divinity and purpose in this life.

Qualities of Luminars

- Powerful, wise presence
- A sense of urgency, feeling like life is short, and living with purpose is a priority
- A feeling of not fitting in with other people or the world in general
- Craving depth rather than superficiality
- Drawn to ancient cultures, spirituality, mystical studies, religion
- May experience perfectionism, self-criticism, self-judgment, not feeling good enough
- Feeling lost, like a stranger in a strange land
- Holding care and love for those who are suffering
- A feeling that there is something important you are here to do with your life
- Strength and courage in the face of challenges
- A connection to sentient beings (animals, plants, trees, crystals)
- Sensitivity; highly developed human abilities such as empathy and extrasensory perception
- Feel your mission is to make the world a better place through healing, art, activism, teaching, engineering, architecture, or other professions.
- Connection to Source/Divine Mother and unseen world
- Memories of past lives as teachers and healers
- Experiences of abuse and trauma
- Feelings of intense anger
- Deep abiding sense of wanting to help the world
- Magnetic presence of love

The Crystars

Stella Maris Speaks:

The second group of light activators we call the Crystars. The Crystars are the most recent generation of light workers, who are relatively new to embodied life on Gaia Earth. We use the word "Crystars" to describe the high vibrational crystalline energy of these beings. The arrival of the Crystars is unprecedented on Earth. In the Buddhist tradition, lamas are reincarnated master souls of the lineage who are found again and again to lead. Crystars are this kind of master soul, great bodhisattvas in human form. What makes them different is that most are not reincarnated, but newly embodied here on Earth. They rest in unity consciousness, born awake and free of earthly constructs. Often they have lived in form in higher-realm worlds, and bring this experience to Earth. Sometimes the Earth can feel dense and shocking for them.

Arriving in greater and greater numbers since the year 2000, this is the newest generation of light activators on Earth. Walt Disney and Nikola Tesla were both Crystar light activators—true creatives and Imagineers of the highest degree, who were early forerunners. We use the words "New World Imagineer" (Imagineer is a term popularized by Walt Disney) to explain the process we will use to heal our world. Crystars will play a crucial role in the vision and creation of new realities on Earth. They hold innate gifts to imagine and engineer radical ideas and solutions.

Crystars hold a pure white light energy within their soul. Their aura energy appears as crystal diamonds with rainbow reflections. Free and awake from birth, they are living examples of love, light, and happiness. They are radiant and magnetic to others because of their pure joy, laughter, and creativity. Crystars can often remember their soul's past, mission, and purpose. All beings are drawn to them, especially Solstar light workers. Crystars are not bound by current culture and are already healed and bright. They are a gift to the Earth and to all of us.

The mission of the Crystars is twofold. They are here to bring forth radical solutions and revolutionary ideas that will heal the Earth and all beings. They are also here to embody their divinity, which will transform everything around them by their mere presence. Great visionaries of the future, they possess incredible gifts and skills that are vital to world healing. They are dreamers, creators, and New World Imagineers of Gaia Earth who resource their power from the divine self within. With the great power of their imagination, they will make rapid changes for the better here. The power of their innate gifts and visionary solutions will quickly heal the Earth and the many problems she is facing. Crystars are great leaders and teachers. They are embodying the leading edge of human evolution, so be open to their perceptions, insights, and ideas. Give them great respect and reverence. As many of them are still children, dissolve old beliefs and paradigms about the treatment of children, that have held humans back for thousands of years.

Crystars exist outside cultural norms and can be misunderstood. They need understanding and guidance from their caregivers and teachers so they do not forget who they are or become lost in cultural conditioning. Because of their extremely developed capacities and sensitivities, they don't always fit in, and can be inappropriately labeled. Parents may think there's something wrong with them and bring them to doctors and specialists who don't understand who they are and why they appear different. These differences can also affect Crystars socially, and they may struggle to "fit in" with other children.

Possessing highly developed extrasensory abilities, Crystars perceive through their attuned senses and intuition. Earthly life can feel very harsh and extreme to them, which can cause difficulties. They are from higher realm worlds, where love is the basis of life. Love is yet to take hold on the Earth as a primary value, so it can be very different than the higher realms they are used to. Parents can best assist Crystars by honoring their differences as unique and beautiful, helping them to develop their gifts, and by building their self-esteem. There will be a future book dedicated solely to understanding and supporting this extraordinary generation.

Qualities of Crystars

- Deep soul wisdom in their eyes
- Usually highly sensitive to sound, touch, taste, smell, and sight, and beyond human senses
- Extrasensory perceptions: They can perceive through their highly attuned senses.
- Keen intuition
- They can be either extremely mellow or high-strung.
- Electrical devices can be affected by their presence.
- Innate wisdom expressed through their teaching and expression
- Exuberance and joy
- Incredibly loving
- Can struggle with social cues and friend issues
- Can seem clueless about social norms and the way humans interact socially
- Sensitive to the energy of people and environments and can respond through change in behavior
- They love creative expression, and will often come up with new ideas and interesting approaches.
- Enjoy dance, music, art, and Nature
- Wisdom beyond their years
- Embody love and light
- A tendency to teach those around them through example and their words
- Signs and synchronicities appear around their birth and life
- Others feel enlightened around them
- Connect easily with animals and the natural world

How Luminars, Crystars, and Solstars Work Together

Stella Maris Speaks:

One of the most important missions of the Luminars is to lead, protect, nurture, and guide the Crystars and Solstars. Luminars are here to nurture and create supportive structures for other light activators. This is a critical time in Earth evolution, truly a time like no other, when we must act as guardians of each other.

Luminars are the forerunners of the Crystar beings. Their presence and light work on Gaia Earth has increased the vibrational frequency to a level where Crystars can take form here. Luminars are wonderful guides, mentors, parents, and teachers of the Crystars. They can create educational and supportive systems that will help Crystars develop their soul presence and unique gifts.

Luminars are also deeply connected to Solstars. Opening to their messages, Luminars can help bring the Solstar wisdom to humanity. Another important role for Luminars is to advocate for the rights of all Solstars for protected habitats and environments.

Although we have differentiated the Starseed light activators for the purpose of your understanding here, these groups are not firmly defined. You can have qualities of more than one group. For example, some light activators may identify with being both Luminar and Crystar, and this is fine. It is not our wish to create labels or categories, just to help you understand yourself and one another better, so you are able to work in partnership.

Principles for Guiding Young Crystars and Luminars

Stella Maris Speaks:

We will now offer brief guidelines for supporting the Crystars. Many of the current parenting ideas and cultural constructs for raising human children will not be helpful in guiding light activators. Mentoring light activators is one of the most important purposes you can undertake. Raising these light beings can be beautiful and challenging.

Stay on Your Evolutionary Path

Honoring your spiritual evolution is the most profound practice you can do to assist light activator children. These beautiful beings have come to Earth through you, and it is a true miracle that they are incarnating here at all. What extraordinary light gifts you have brought through your physical form and awakened consciousness! Give yourself a big hug and exuberant love for this great contribution. At the moment of your child's birth, thousands of angels were singing in the heavens, celebrating the miracle of his or her life on Earth. Honor yourself for being awake and conscious enough to bring these beautiful souls to the Earth.

Your spiritual evolution is the most important gift you can give your children for their own healing. The quality of your inner light transfers automatically to them. So if you engage in spiritual practices that balance and support your life, they will receive the benefit of your transmission instantaneously.

When your child incarnates, you automatically transfer your ancestral lineage, DNA, and other issues to your children as an energetic inheritance. If you consciously heal and transform these energy patterns, your child inherits something new and the ability to transcend limitations. We invite you to take radical responsibility for your own healing and vibratory state so you can help stop negative human cycles for future generations. Your healing will heal your children, your ancestors, and descendants.

Parenthood is not a reason to stop taking care of yourself. In fact, self-care is more important than ever as a parent. We invite you to lead by energetic example, showing your children how to live a truly human and beautiful life. Teach them to follow their hearts, offer their gifts, and live their divine purpose. Do not put your own needs on hold, buying into the old belief that once you become a parent you must sacrifice your own needs. This is unnecessary, and detrimental to all. Your personal evolution is the greatest gift you can give them. Show them how you embrace your Higher Self and how to gracefully live a human experience. Light activator children can accurately perceive if you are saying one thing and doing another, so live with integrity, aligning your words, actions, and energy.

We honor your choice of spiritual path, for all paths lead to the same truth. Whatever your choice, share your spirituality with your child. They are already in an awakened state, and they benefit from experiences of spirituality and love. Share what is most dear to your heart, your beliefs, your values. Share your daily practices. Do not assume children can't receive spiritual truths because of their physical age. This is simply not true. Read together, listen to music, connect with art, teach them meditation and how to listen to their hearts.

Create a Peaceful Home

Light activator children can be extremely sensitive to environments because of their highly developed sensory perceptions. All of their senses—sight, hearing, taste, touch, and smell—are highly attuned. They may have ESP, visions, or prophetic dreams, or see energy fields and other beings who exist without physical form. They may perceive information and energy from others that is beyond your perception. Validate their experiences and do not dismiss them as unreal or imaginary. We invite you to be willing to expand your awareness and consider their perceptions real, or at least real for them. Because of their high sensitivity, world experiences can feel harsh or disconcerting for them. Please offer comfort and understanding in response to their needs. Create a soothing home environment that is peaceful and safe. Let your home be a sanctuary of love and light for your child. Psychically clean your home on a regular basis, which means regularly clearing the energy within your home with sage, cedar, sweet grass, rosewater, or other materials that work best for you. Create intentional spaces that are protected and energetically clear. When your baby is first born, take great care in sheltering them, and try not to take them out in the world for at least six to eight weeks. Provide a calming environment where they can transition from the womb space to your home space. Prepare a home environment that is soothing to their sight, hearing, taste, smell, and touch.

Provide Opportunities to Be in the Natural World

Give light activator children many opportunities to connect with the natural world. Create ceremonies related to the change of seasons, and teach them how to ground themselves on the Earth. Provide opportunities for them to connect to life in many forms: animals, plants, and rocks. Help them to have relationships with Solstars by providing animal companions or opportunities for them to interact with animals.

Take them hiking or camping and revel together in Nature's majesty. Grow a garden and teach them about their relationship with food, Nature, devas, and fairies. Show them the majestic beauty of Gaia and their deep connection to the Earth. Teach them about how to connect to the elements of wind, earth, fire, and water. Experience the sacred night, the magic of the moon and stars. Discover new and unexpected natural surprises. Bring them to the water often—to rivers, lakes, streams, or the ocean—for water brings them great healing. Travel and take them to special sacred locations on Earth. Deeply connect them with Gaia Earth and all of her beauty.

Protect and Guard Their Magical Childhood

Childhood is a most precious stage of human development for light activators. Protect and guard their magical childhood. We suggest you avoid trying to make your child "grow up" or act like a miniature adult. Honor the wonder and magic of this time, when the human connection between heaven and Earth is strongest. Carefully choose schools that honor childhood and understand the important stages of child development. Assess the underlying philosophy and approach of your child's school. For example, Waldorf education, an approach by Rudolf Steiner, creates a holistic approach to teaching children that honors their head, hands, heart, and soul.

Many of the education systems on Earth are outdated and are still teaching from a mechanistic perspective. We call for a complete transformation of human educational systems, based on the understanding of how to raise truly evolved and awakened human beings. Education should not be a way to perpetuate outdated beliefs, limited thinking, and indoctrination. Instead, it should encourage revolutionary thinking, original ideas, and out-of-the-box thinking. Music, art, and creativity are incredibly important to the Crystars. Match your child's soul essence with the right school.

Light Activator Children and Technology

Technology is a powerful tool, and light activator children will often know how to use it intuitively. We advise you to wait as long as possible to introduce screens and technology into your child's life. Technology has many benefits, most specifically its ability to connect people through cyberspace. Light activators may use technology extensively in their future, but if it is introduced too soon it can be disabling, stunting their highly evolved abilities. We recommend limiting your child's time in front of a screen during the ages of zero to ten and minimizing screen time in general.

We also encourage you to shelter your child from the Internet, world news, and social media for as long as possible. Do not share information with them about negative world events until they are old enough to process what they are hearing. Light activator children can be extremely sensitive, and learning about negative world events can create fears and anxiety that are unnecessary and detrimental to their development.

We invite you to teach them how to use technology as a tool in service to the heart. Explain how to avoid the pitfalls of screen addiction, media influence, and negative marketing. Teach them how to be independent and critical thinkers who can discern when they are trying to be controlled or influenced. Once they begin to use technology, show them how to regularly disconnect from it, especially through your example. Notice when you are using your computer, iPad, or cell phone, and curb the need to do so when you are with your children.

Technology can adversely affect human development, and you will discover this in the future. You are currently embracing this powerful tool without knowledge of its impact and without regard for your protection. Millions of people may be negatively impacted by the use of technology. So we urge you to proceed with great caution when it comes to your children and mainstream media, apps, and games. Again, we are not saying all technology is bad, just that it is not best for developing light activators.

Screen devices are highly addictive and can impede your child's brain development, crippling their important pathways to the higher dimensions of reality. Screens remove your child from real world experience and place them in a disconnected world created by others. The average human child spends eight hours a day on screens and devices. Screens and devices are highly addictive, and the nature of this will be revealed more and more in time. Addiction to technology is real and very dangerous, especially for the light activator child. It can take away your child's innate ability to rest in the present moment, sustain attention, and use their imagination, and also their ability to anchor and ground in their physical body.

To live their greatest purpose, your child will need the ability to use all facets of their being, especially their imagination. Technology can distract and cripple their natural visionary ability. Old power structures would prefer to keep your child removed from reality, trapped in virtual worlds and rendering them powerless and under control. If they get lost in virtual worlds, their gifts will be stifled. Children who spend too much time using screen devices often will not develop their truly human capacity to use their intuition and senses. It is critical that you protect your child's visionary ability for their future life purpose.

Help for Guiding Light Activators with Technology

- Help your child delve into their six senses and beyond by playing creative games that involved all six senses.
- Provide opportunities for art projects, creativity, music, and dance. If they are bored, don't worry. Boredom is the birthplace of creativity.
- Read guided journey and visualization stories to help them practice using their imagination.
- Create individually tailored visionary journeys for your child, based on the challenges they are experiencing.
- When your child is struggling, create a story to address their challenges and to provide insight or healing. The healing power of story is incredible and has been used throughout human time.
- Have your child spend time in Nature cultivating their inner being and sense of wonder.
- Limit time on technology, screens, and devices, being especially vigilant in the years of early childhood development, ages zero to ten.
- Create a clear contract on how and when they can use technology. Avoid the use of social media for as long as possible, and have them use it with clear guidelines.

Remind Light Activators of Who They Really Are

From the moment of their birth, remind your child of who they really are: an angelic being of light and love. Share with them how their presence heals the world, and their true identity as one divine being in human form. Don't let them forget they are on an important mission here. Provide opportunities for your children to delve into their interests at different ages and stages. Observe who they are, and match their daily experience to their soul expression. Even if you do not understand why your child is asking to participate in something or why they are obsessed with a certain topic, trust that your child's Higher Self is guiding them clearly. Do your best to honor their needs, and have faith in a great plan for their life. Your child is aware of exactly what is needed for their evolution at every age.

Enhance your child's knowledge about energy. Crystars are born with an innate ability to work within the energetic realms. Give them opportunities to do so. Demonstrate how they can direct healing energy through their hands with the intention to heal. Good resources for accessing information about energy are Healing Touch, Therapeutic Touch, Reiki, and other energy work approaches. Honor their perceptions of energy, and show your child how to work with negative or harsh energies. Teach them about their aura, the energy field that surrounds their body, and how to activate protective boundaries around them. Show them how to use psychic protection during the day and at night. Give them ways to understand their extra-sensory perceptions of energy. Validate their perceptions and experiences of the energy field in places and with people.

Teach them about color therapy, energy healing, and the chakra system. The chakra system is group of energy centers in the body that direct energy flow. There are seven main chakras that align with the spine, starting from the crown of the head and ending at the base of the spine. They look like spinning wheels of color. Purple is the crown, indigo is the on the forehead, the throat is blue, the heart is green, the solar plexus is yellow, the sacral is orange, the root or base of the spine is red. Blocked chakra flow can result in illness, so it's important to keep these energy centers flowing, and for light activator children to know how to balance their energy.

Laugh and Play Together

Children are expert teachers in the art of fun, laughter, and play. Seize the opportunity to relish these qualities in their presence. Learn from them about how to be silly and laugh. Let them teach you how to regain the quality of levity and brightness in your life. Be free of the constraints of your adult self. Raising a light activator child is the perfect opportunity to reconnect with your own inner child. Most adults have lost the connection to their inner child after being taught they needed "to grow up" to effectively function in the world. This is one of the greatest lies the world tells you, for your inner child is the steward of your inner joy, wonder, delight, and excitement. When you are cut off from this pure part of yourself, you become dull and lifeless. Reconnect to this part of you as you play with your children. Their laughter and delight can activate and heal you! Your joy can heal them! Play is one of the most enjoyable activities you can do together.

Honor Your Child as Your Great Teacher

Honor your child as one of your greatest teachers. Light activator children are embodying the leading edge of human evolution. Listen to their perceptions, beliefs, and insights. Honor their wisdom deeply. Be open to their ideas, and see the world through their eyes. Allow your eyes to light up when they walk into the room. Love them unconditionally.

Speak to your child as the evolved being that they are. Treat them with respect. Listen to their experiences and perceptions. Never assume they are ignorant, based on their physical age. A reverent approach to child-raising can help break the long-time cultural construct that has been responsible for violating and disrespecting children for far too long. This old belief views children as ignorant, bothersome, a pain, and pawns for economic gain or a burden. Remember the saying, "a child must be seen and not heard"? This view of children must be changed. See, hear, and listen to your children. Be aware of these cultural patterns within you and actively seek to transform them in relationship with your child.

Honor your child for their inner light and remind them often that they have come to Earth for an important purpose. Let go of the expectation that they will fit into the world the way that it is, and embrace them as the bringer of change. Provide opportunities for them to build upon their natural gifts and talents, as well as opportunities to develop new strengths. Give them opportunities to learn skills that follow their unique interests. Assist with problem-solving if they ask. Give them opportunities for responsibility and independence.

Remind them of their inner wise self, who is available to help them at any time. You can teach them how to listen to their heart and follow their intuitions and feelings. Teach them how to become still, breathe, and listen within through yoga, meditation, journaling, and other centering techniques.

Light Activator Children and Healthcare

Light activator children can be extremely sensitive to modern Western medicine. Design a medical approach that works best with your child's body, mind, and soul. Homeopathy can be extremely effective, as well as other forms of vibrational medicine. Vibrational medicine is an approach to healthcare that understands the energy resonance your body is made of. There are many living remedies that can be used for healing, including the use of sound, plants, crystals, acupuncture, elixirs, sunlight, and food.

Be very vigilant about the quality of food and water you give to your child. Light activators can have more food sensitivities and can have stronger reactions to chemicals and GMOs in food. We recommend non-GMO, organic diets for young light activators. Teach them about food as medicine and that their relationships with food and water can be the building blocks of their health. We recommend you do all of the above for yourself too!

The Solstars

We are light keepers
Who appear in many forms
Trees, animals, flowers, and stones
Wise and benevolent beings,
Who give you our hearts
Activating universal love and unity consciousness,
The greatest powers on Earth
We are deeply aware, intelligent beyond your understanding
Conscious and feeling beings
Who are entitled to life and safe homes
We are deeply connected to our mother, Gaia Earth
Light Messengers of her wisdom
Let us assist you
We offer many teachings to share with humanity
If you will only listen

Stella Maris Speaks:

Solstars are sentient being light activators who work in alignment with the Divine Mother and Gaia Earth. What differentiates us from other animals or plants is that we are aware of our choice to anchor unity consciousness here. We remember our purpose and offer our oneness wisdom. All creatures on Gaia Earth belong to each other and are members of Indra's web, a vast structure of connection. We help to maintain the web of balance and understand that great harmony is possible through Gaia's brilliantly designed systems.

One of our important missions is to work in partnership with human light activators to bring healing to this world. We also protect and speak for the many sentient beings who live on Earth. We are born in a myriad of forms—animals, trees, flowers, stones, and plants. We may not speak in your language, but we understand your communication to us. Can you hear our communication to you?

Life has existed on Gaia Earth for four billion years in balance. In a short span of time, humans have disrupted the natural harmony on Earth to such a degree that all of life is in jeopardy. You are part of a vast network of light activators who can reinstate this balance. Together we can realign the Earth's balance through embracing the divine feminine approach to life. This approach holds the values of listening, connection, love, acceptance, mutual support, unity, empathy, caring for future generations, and nurturing of all of life. The feminine fosters interdependence and community.

The Solstar light activators exist in unity consciousness, in natural alignment with Source. As guides and companions, we activate this same consciousness within you. We can take the form of any animal, tree, or flower. We are both domestic and wild. There are four groups of Solstars we would like to speak with you about, for they are wisdom keepers of unity consciousness: redwood trees, whales, bees, and dolphins. These Solstars are keepers of an energetic planetary grid which maintains balance and health for the Earth. The grid is a sacred geometric structure that keeps Gaia Earth's energy flowing. The grid has sacred locations worldwide, each operating as Gaia Earth's chakras or doorways to divine Source.

The redwoods are ancient wise beings who anchor the heavenly realms on Earth. Their lineage extends back millions of years, and they have existed as wisdom keepers for many generations. The tops of their branches extend into the light of higher realms, while their roots anchor this energy on Earth. They exist in groves of connection, their roots intertwined in the soil, where they send and receive messages. Redwood beings anchor the light of oneness on the Earth plane and should be protected and honored. You can think of them as tending the doorway to the crown chakra of Gaia Earth, along with the mountains.

The whales migrate along the Earth's energy lines, keeping the balance and flow of the planet. They are amplifiers of unity consciousness, singing songs of beauty and healing. They are guardians of the Earth's throat chakras. The power of their voices keeps balance and alignment in the great waters. Potent whale songs transform and awaken reality itself. The dolphins and whales are intimately connected as family and share a divine purpose. We often work together to bring healing to all of life.

The bees exist in a "we consciousness," a unity existence where many individual bees operate as one being. They are a wonderful example of how many individuals can live as one being. With the extraordinary ability to use their multidimensional perceptions, they serve the third eye chakras of Earth. Their complexity and brilliance blesses all of us. Bees are light emissaries between the human and plant world who facilitate the emergence of life through their selfless service. If you listen closely, you can hear their chants and songs of oneness.

Dolphins have an important role as Solstar light activators. We are your ancient family and guardians and are uniquely suited to work with you for planetary healing. We steward the energetic portals where the higher realms connect to Earth. As specially appointed guardians of the sacred element of water, we purify and balance the electrical structure within water. Our presence has stopped catastrophic events from occurring, as we are a stabilizing force for Gaia Earth's body and energetic systems. As guardians of the water ley lines, we are keepers of Gaia's heart chakra. This is why our Hawaiian name means "keepers of unconditional love." We are emissaries of the heart who amplify the energy of love through our unified consciousness. We also maintain a clear connection with other star system civilizations and anchor their higher consciousness and wisdom on Earth.

We are living examples of how to embody unity consciousness and balance within form. Your scientists are only beginning to understand the highly evolved nature of dolphins. Living in oneness consciousness, we radiate the pure joy of the

Source energy. We are evolved beings who embody perfect feminine and masculine balance, brain alignment, and energy flow. We hold vibrational patterns and frequencies of light for human evolution on Gaia Earth, and because we are so closely related, we are uniquely suited to help you. We have not forgotten our true nature, and we exist in natural flow. Wise keepers of how to live in the present, we hold the divine feminine medicine for healing through the power of connection, love, and unity. We are honored to join with you as partners and friends. This is what we have been waiting for.

You can experience the deepest part of your humanity through your interactions with Solstar beings and the natural world. We hope you can now see the important purposes Solstars are undertaking here. Look at us with love and admiration, as you watch the migration of the whales and birds. Honor the ancient redwood trees, who anchor heaven's light. Inhale the sweet scent and magical tones of blooming flower, and listen closely to the buzz of the bees.

Solstars also include mystical creatures, beings that are no longer embodied on Earth. This includes dragons, unicorns, griffins, fairies, and others. There was a time when the mystical ones graced the Earth with their physical form, but it became unsafe, so they migrated to higher vibrational realities. You can catch a glimpse, if they want to reveal themselves to you. The mystical Solstars are happy to offer their guidance, if you would like their help. Dragons, fairies, and unicorns are especially interested in helping with the current awakening on Earth. They bring you the gifts of divine creation and leadership. Now that you know they are here to support you, you may notice them showing up in your life through stories and symbols.

We encourage you to practice communicating with Solstar beings. We are in constant telepathic communication and would love to share more messages with all of you! By healing yourself and remembering who you are, your intuitive channels will be cleared and opened. Once your telepathic abilities are activated, you will be able to clearly hear the messages of the Solstars, even when you are not in their physical presence. You can start by opening communication with the Solstars closest in your life. Sit under your favorite tree, center yourself, and listen. Try communicating through imagery with your companion cat or dog. You will receive their communication through words, pictures, or images, or through direct downloads to your heart.

As you develop your listening capacity, you will be able to have conversations with trees, stones, and animals. Everything will come alive, and you will receive incredible help and wisdom. Interspecies communication will happen easily as you evolve, for it is an ability you are all born with. As you are able to communicate more effectively, our partnership will become stronger. All light activators are here to work together to restore balance to our collective habitat and environmental systems.

Human beings were designed as telepathic beings who can easily connect to each other and all of life. You were not designed to be alone and separate in the isolation of your ego mind. The modern-day experiences of isolation are creating unhappiness and in extreme cases causing human beings to lose their sanity. Unity connects you to all of life and restores your knowledge that you are a very important part of an intricate web of life. You belong here. You are loved. From the perspective of connection, you will recognize the impact of your consciousness on all beings.

Divine feminine consciousness restores love as your primary operating system, instead of fear. Existing in unity, you can instantly know the impact of your every choice on all life. We invite you to this experience. Claim your divine inheritance. You are divine beings in human form. Return to unity and live an awakened life. Let us work in partnership, for together we can birth the new paradigms and living stories on Gaia Earth by weaving a new and brilliant Indra's web. This is what our beloved Gaia desperately needs. She will now speak in her own words.

Gaia Earth Speaks

Beloved Child:

The time has come for the next stage of my evolution. I am entering a new stage of my highest divine service as a planetary being. I have provided you with a home where you can experience life in form. I have given you everything you need, in hope that it will assist you with your greatest evolution. I simply ask this of you: Remember your connection to me, treat me with love and respect, and honor my body as your beautiful home.

Your journey is one of personal and collective transformation, so it not only includes yourself, it includes the welfare and evolution of all beings here. In recent years, humans have created a destructive imbalance in my body that negatively impacts all of my children. My beautiful tree beings have been cut down. My stone people have been mined to extinction. My water and air is polluted. Food is grown with poisons and toxins, contaminating the soil and groundwater. My animals are disappearing at an alarming rate. The systems I created to keep life balanced are severely damaged and broken. All of my children are suffering because of humans' unbalanced and destructive way of life. Humans are now threatening the existence of all life on my body, and Indra's web is becoming weak.

You must change your current ways, or the result will be the end of the human experience here. Our time together grows short, and I speak to you with urgency. Please begin powerful steps to restore my balance. I call on every being to take action through the power of their heart and in partnership with my beloved Solstars. Work collectively and quickly, dear ones. The Solstar beings remember the returning way of wisdom and balance. Listen and learn from them, and make different choices. They can teach you how to live in alignment. . . . The time is here. Come to my aid. Miracles are possible. I love you more than words can express, my beautiful children. Thank you for your willingness to help me. —**Gaia Earth**

Qualities of Solstars

- Deep wisdom in their eyes
- Embodiment of love
- Living in conscious alignment with the natural world
- Connected with their wild nature
- Archetypal animals throughout history. (For example, the dragon, unicorn, turtle, and griffin are considered powerful magical animals in China.)
- Emanations of peace and love
- Their presence transforms
- Equanimity
- Living in balance with Gaia Earth
- Follow natural flow and rhythms
- Unity consciousness keepers
- Conscious awareness of mission and purpose
- Emissaries of the light

Chapter 8
New World Imagineers

You are ready to emerge
You have waited through the dark night with faith and patience
Holding hope in the depths of your heart
It is time
Remember . . . Awaken . . . Emerge . . .
The moment has arisen
There is no greater purpose than the flowering of your true self
Unfurl your petals
Your magnificence is exactly what the world needs
You are a Divine Imagineer, a Master Cocreator
Ground yourself deeply on Gaia Earth
Open your Starseed light
And Bloom!

What Is a New World Imagineer?

Stella Maris Speaks:

A New World Imagineer is a being who aligns with their Higher Self and highest divine purpose, to create new world paradigms, systems, and consciousness on Earth. We use the term "New World Imagineer" to convey the process of creation in partnership with Source. Creation is made possible through the high vibrations of love and light. By combining two words, "imagine" and "engineer," the word "Imagineer" is created. We acknowledge that this term is familiar, as it was made popular by Walt Disney, a Crystar being who understood the genius of this creative process.

The word "imagine" speaks to your creative ability to envision and form an image of something you have not yet experienced. Using your imagination, you can create new ideas that do not yet exist in the world. An engineer is someone who invents, designs, improves, and innovates. Engineers bring design into form. So Imagineering is the process of using your divine imagination and taking action to manifest it into form. You have the ability to listen within, envision and imagine, and to actualize your divinely guided ideas to create a new world. The term "New World Imagineer" can refer to an individual or can describe the action of Imagineering.

Within the word imagine is the word "magi." The Magi are an ancient group of wise beings who know how to live in balance and hold universal secrets of transformation, alchemy, and magical manifestation. Some Magi exist in the higher realms and other star systems, and others have chosen to incarnate on Earth. These wise and empowered beings access the magic of their divine self, laws of physics, and divine alchemy to create. All humans are gifted with the ability of the Magi; we invite you to remember your own magical inheritance. Work your magic!

New World Imagineering is the key to creating our peaceful collective future. A practice utilized in many ancient cultures on Earth for manifestation, this process unlocks your unlimited creative potential through a partnership with unified consciousness. There is an abundance of ideas available, if only you know where to resource them. Light activators are here to work together in alignment with the Divine Mother, the Source of all life, who is available to co-create new divinely guided ideas and realities. Sourcing ideas from unity consciousness, the creative intelligent field of life is how creative solutions and revolutionary ideas are born.

The vibrational energy behind the New World Imagineer movement is one of joy, magic, laughter, love, and light, for these energies offer creative brilliance with ease and grace. The Beauty Way frequencies can easily manifest new realities and structures. As you access the power of your Higher Self, you can do extraordinary things. Please remember that the presence of your Higher Self, just your being, will also create planetary healing. Follow your bliss and find others to help magnify the power of collective intention. The possibilities are endless if you resource divine solutions for world problems.

As a New World Imagineer, you can literally shape and redesign Earth reality through your intention, imagination, and joy. Access your inner light and creative intelligence to bring forward revolutionary solutions. You are original and can see new ways when others can't, for you exist outside of societal norms and old constructs. Higher realm consciousness can heal Gaia Earth and all of her inhabitants. As you contribute to the healing of Gaia Earth, this will also precipitate healing for other galaxies, planets, and star systems.

You Are a New World Imagineer

Stella Maris Speaks:

You are a visionary. You are the ones the Earth has been waiting for. You have infinite resources within your Higher Self to anchor unity consciousness. You have the power to bring your divinely guided visions into reality for the good of all beings. You are a brilliant Starseed who holds the keys to the healing, awakening, and reconstruction of the planet. You are a New World Imagineer, a true creative of unlimited potential. Your gifts and imagination will change everything for the better. Your individual and collective offerings will heal and resurrect Gaia Earth and all of life. Rise up together to bless this world and all of her inhabitants. And so it is, and so it will be.

Visionary Empowerment Statement
for New World Imagineers

By Stella Maris

Speak Aloud:

I am a visionary. I am the one the world has waited for. My Higher Self anchors unity consciousness and guides my way. I dedicate my life to my divinity, sharing my gifts, and embracing my highest divine purpose. Existing as my true divine self, I radiate resonant waves of healing light and love to all. I am vast and hold the seeds of all possibility. Imagining what is possible, I bring my divinely inspired visions into reality. I am the heart and key to the healing, awakening, and reconstruction of Gaia Earth. I hold within me true creativity and unlimited potential. My gifts and my vision will change everything for the better. I work in partnership with other light activators to heal the Earth and all beings. I fully commit my life to this great purpose. I honor the divinity within me and within all of life. I am a living prayer and miracle. My life is incredibly important for the revolution of love. I walk the Beauty Way, sowing seeds of love, awakening, and enlightenment wherever I go. I am the blessing and the blessed. I am a brilliant shooting star for the dawn of this new age. I am a New World Imagineer. And so it is.

Being a New World Imagineer Means Living as Your Divine Self

Stella Maris Speaks:

We invite you to recognize that it is time to stop living in ways that no longer suit you. It is time to live as your divine Higher Self. You have been learning and growing for a long time, and now it is time to embody your learning.

You are a multidimensional, spiritual being of light. A beautifully unique soul, your essence and love consciousness brings light to places of darkness. When you commit to embodying your true Higher Self, radical positive changes occur in your life. Alignment, synchronicity, magic, and grace become everyday experiences. Your connection to the Divine Mother will radiate peaceful vibrations to all.

As a New World Imagineer, you will be guided to create many things, but remember, your life is not about simply doing. It is, most importantly, about the cultivation of your being. It is time to cultivate your high vibrational qualities of joy, play, laughter, and light.

As you rest in divine oneness, you will discover and receive divinely guided ideas, inspiration, and creativity. The divine feminine creates from this rich inner world. As you connect to your true self, your radiance will transform your life and the lives of those who come into contact with you. Be willing to rest often in solitude and silence, listening to the Divine Mother and envisioning the possible. This means setting aside time every day to listen, so you can hear the whispering of your sacred heart. From this place of quietness, you will receive your divine assignments. Arising out of this deep rest, silence, and solitude, you will discover your true unlimited creative potential.

You are a trailblazer, one who embodies a new way of life on Gaia Earth. We invite you to exist as the being of light and love that you are. Release your cultural conditioning of doing and striving. Rest in the unknown divine feminine consciousness with faith in the heart of all. Remember how wonderful you are. You are an indescribable gift. You are everything wonderful. You are a beautiful soul. You are sweet sauce and honey pie all wrapped in a human suit. You are the bee's knees and the sugar pie darling of our hearts. We love you beyond your imaginings.

You have the opportunity to create new living stories through your life. A new way of being human on this Earth. Your life can be a living, breathing masterpiece, an alive story being experienced and lived within the Divine Mother. Your living story is your greatest contribution; what story will you tell through your human life? What will be your demonstration of love? As you live in this new way, you become an inspiration for others to also live with more joy, beauty, connection, and peace. You are a master creatrix who can decide to inhabit the life of your dreams. Gone is the notion that you need to suffer for what you would like; you can rest in your divinity and enjoy your life.

Watch how you magnetize everything you need for your great purpose here. Conserve your energy and choose to spend your days engaged in what matters most to you. Offer your attention to projects that energize you. Ask yourself: Does this activity energize me or deplete me? Choose to participate in those projects, experiences, and activities that bring you the greatest joy, inspiration, and excitement.

It is time for New World Imagineers to come out of the trenches and experience freedom from the old structures that have bound them. You are here to create, not to be trapped by what currently exists. Hold the vision of what can be. Make life changes that let more light in. We invite you to do this for yourself and on behalf of all life. It is time. We invite you to trust, receive, and accept the great calling of your most beautiful life. Your self activation will reshape your life into a masterpiece that reflects the true nature of your Higher Self.

Every New World Imagineer Has Unique Gifts and Offerings

Stella Maris Speaks:

We consider every being who wants to participate in the Earth's great awakening a New World Imagineer. Human New World Imagineers are present across all specialties, fields of study, and professions. We will speak more about this topic in the future, but for now would like to offer a glimpse of the many specialties of Imagineers. What all Imagineers have in common is their sincere desire to heal the world and birth new realities on Earth. When Imagineers work together, the power of collective intention makes everything possible. We invite you to create vast networks which will connect New World Imagineers from around the world so they can align their gifts and make rapid global shifts. All of these specialties overlap with one another. We are offering this idea as a general guideline.

New World Imagineer Specialties

Artists: Creatives, Musicians, Actors, Writers, Painters, Architects, Landscapers, and Storytellers

Healers: All Healers, Doctors, Environmentalists, Activists

Inventors: Engineers, Visionaries, Mathematicians, Scientists, Artists

Leaders: Consensus Builders, Mediation Specialists, Leaders of Divine Government, Community Organizers, Advocates

Teachers: Messengers, Teachers, Channels, Visionaries, Intuitives, Revolutionaries, Spiritual Guides

Divine Guiding Principles of Imagineers

Return to Oneness

Stella Maris Speaks:

As light messengers, we are in a constant state of immersion with unity consciousness. We invite you to return to this place, the warm embrace of the Divine Mother, where you can rest in your inherent oneness. Swim consciously in the sea of being, floating weightless and formless in the source of your being, where infinite wisdom abides. In the depth of this oneness, you can dwell in the endless ocean of your true self. This dimensionless state is where you can draw energy and ideas to create new realities on Earth. In unity consciousness, you are truly one with all living creatures and the entire universe, and can access ways to bring all the highest good.

As a New World Imagineer, you recognize all of life as a divine creation, arising from the one Source. The word "namaste" captures the essence of this idea—it means the light within me acknowledges and honors the light within you. We are a network of living beings, many forms of one being. It is the great paradox, to seemingly be individuals, yet in truth be one.

All beings have an important place within this network of light. A change in one living system impacts all other systems on Gaia Earth. Your healing creates restoration for all. Just like one drop of water sends our concentric circles into a lake, your new vibration will affect the entire world. Your every thought, vibration, and action affects the whole. Walk in your divine awareness, holding compassion for all of creation.

Live Your Divinity

Now that you remember who you really are, we invite you to engage in daily practices that will help you live your divinity. As a Starseed light activator on Earth, your brilliant inner star can guide your life. You will never know who you really are, based on information from the outside world. Discovering your true self can be supported by the practices of inquiry and self-knowing. We invite you to truly know the grace within. Your heart is your guide.

There are many practices offered that can assist you with inner discovery, such as meditation, art, dance, music, travel, and yoga. All paths lead to the same truth of your brilliance. We honor all spiritual and religious paths and honor your choices to access whatever is most helpful for your journey. Time in Nature, ceremony, meditation, music, sound, and art are all helpful for quieting your mind and connecting you to the Divine Mother and higher realms.

Begin by stating your intention or wish to discover your true self and to integrate your Higher Self more fully. Ask for help if you like; the angels, guides, and ascended masters are surrounding you in every moment. We are here to assist you, but must respect your free will and choice. If you ask for help, it will be immediately given. As you commit to the discovery of yourself and activate your channels of awareness, you will notice the signs of how you are deeply guided through alignments and synchronicity. Listen to and engage life by noticing these synchronicities and repeated signs that life is reflecting to you.

Become a great listener. The outside world is filled with distractions and noise. How can you make space for silence, solitude, and listening in your life? How will your still, small voice be heard, unless you create time for it to speak? When you engage in listening practices daily, you can hear from the depths of your soul.

Restore Your Inner Children to Activate Your Creativity and Magical Manifestation Power

Stella Maris Speaks:

You have important allies within that innately know how to be in joyous flow: your inner children. Yes, you have many inner children within, and they have the innate ability to find wonder in the ordinary, magic in the air, and delight in the joy of just being alive. You may believe you no longer have inner children within you, but they are there, holding different feelings and past experiences. You have many psychological parts that come together to make up your "ego self" personality. These parts can become lost, ignored, or frightened by experiences of trauma and difficulty. Inner child healing is a multifaceted journey that is extremely important to your evolution into a fully evolved human being. The journey back to your inner children is not always easy, but it is necessary to find them within you, because they have never lost their imagination and belief in magic. Your inner children are the ones we invite you to remember because they hold the keys to your creative abilities.

One of these inner children is your phoenix child. This is the child within who has never been touched by any experience or challenge. He or she holds the resonance of your pure innocence and remains intact, pure, and true. Reconnect to this precious one within. See the world through the eyes of the phoenix child. Celebrate your one precious life with joy and exhilaration. Laugh again. Discover the wonder of your life. Your phoenix child holds the keys to your healing and empowerment as a magical, divine co-creator. Your phoenix child is your creative and revolutionary leader. The phoenix child is where your true New World Imagineer power lies, jump-starting your highest evolution. Invite him or her to rise as a phoenix from the ashes and become the guiding force of your life.

We suggest you become the most amazing inner mother and inner father to your inner children. Be the best parent you can be for yourself. Release built-up resentment toward your parents, knowing they did the best they could from their level of consciousness. Your Higher Self can be the parent you never had. Be willing to journey with this part of you and to create space for your inner children to heal.

Embrace the Beauty Way to Activate Your Joy, Creativity, Laughter, Love, Light, and Play

When you live the Beauty Way, you embrace life with:

- Unbridled creativity
- Connection to Source, the Divine Mother, your True and Higher Self
- Moment-to-moment awareness of your heart's guidance
- Raucous laughter
- Overflowing joy
- Clear intuition
- Maximum bliss
- Beauty wherever you go, through kindness or creation
- An ability to see the oneness of all life
- Everyday magic and synchronicity
- A creative alliance with the Universe/Source
- Extreme gratitude
- Unspeakable radiance
- The power of love
- Curiosity and wonder
- Access to your inner wisdom on a daily basis
- Solitude and silence
- Loads of fun
- Self-love
- Connection and empathy
- Divine feminine consciousness

Living the Beauty Way is a powerful way you can contribute to planetary healing and awakening. By embracing your love and light, you create a gateway to your Higher Self and the creative powers of the entire universe. You are able to dance your life into being through your luminosity. Your life becomes a living prayer, a work of art, a unique song that radiates high vibrational frequencies to the entire world. You become a light activator. This is truly why you have come. Remember, your Beauty Way is unique to you, because it is designed by your divine blueprint. You are invited to create your most beautiful life, your melody, your artistic masterpiece.

Your Higher Self naturally exists in beauty, resonating with the vibrations of joy, laughter, love, light, and play. Anchoring these energies is an important part of your purpose here on Earth. The more you embody love and light, the more you heal yourself and others who come in contact with you. Be the beauty of your true self. Bless all, love all, live as the being of light that you are. Have fun living your life, laugh often and loudly. Play at every opportunity. Dance the whisperings of your soul. Create beauty wherever you go. Live joyfully!

What a wonderful assignment, right? Can you see yourself telling another: "I'm sorry, I'm no longer spending my time suffering, instead I am being the most joyous, loving, light-filled person I can. I'm just too busy following my bliss to have time for anything else!" We do not mean that you should ignore or avoid your true human feelings. They still need to be felt, embraced, and honored! You will experience all of your human feelings and return again and again to your natural state of joy and happiness. You will cultivate your ability to hold infinite love and joy in your heart.

Imagine the Possible and Take Action
on Your Divinely Guided Ideas

Your creativity is waiting for your attention and time. We invite you to develop your visionary ability and imagination, for the world needs the star gifts embedded in your heart. As a New World Imagineer, you are a visionary leader. Develop and nurture your inner vision, and allow your imagination to play. You have an entire world of ideas inside of you. Give yourself the space, solitude, and silence to hear them. Explore your inner world.

A powerful force for good and healing, your contribution can have a real and immediate impact upon the world. Remember to use your phoenix child power and access the genius who can turn a tree into a goddess or a white horse into a unicorn. The power of your imagination can transform anything through the alchemy of divine magic. Ask for clear vision and spiritual sight.

You are a unique creation, and you hold the entire universe within. Co-create in partnership with the universe. A common block you may have is believing you are not artistic or are limited in your creativity. Old beliefs of not feeling good enough or not loving yourself only serve to block the divine solutions from coming through you. As you heal, you unleash your creative powers. We are here to tell you that you possess unlimited creative potential. Unleashing your creativity will bring you great joy and bring you into alignment with your purpose. All ideas are built on others, just like patterns are unique and the same. Be the original that you are!

Once you have envisioned or imagined your ideas, take steps to manifest them. There has been much written about how to manifest in the world. Here is our guidance: Once you receive an idea from the Source, hold the creation in your mind's eye and feel your inner love, joy, appreciation, and gratitude in your heart. Envision your idea or solution existing in the physical world, created through the power of love. Breathe deeply and see all the details clearly. Infuse your creation with light as you breathe in and out. Use your five senses to breathe your creation into life. What does it look like? How does it smell? How does it taste? What do you hear? What do you feel? What do you want to bless this project with? After creating a tangible vision, release your creation to the Source. Turn it over to the one divine being and let go. This is a way you can enter into a co-creative partnership with life itself.

Watch for synchronicity. Synchronicity is when the inner and outer worlds align, creating events or experiences that affirm and support you. It is a way to gauge if you are truly operating in flow and divine alignment. People and situations can come to you effortlessly. You may notice recurrent signs or communications from life itself. All of life will align to assist you in your divinely guided purpose.

Activate your vision through action. As you receive guidance and suggestions from life, follow through on them. Each day, prioritize what is most important to you, and show up with commitment to your purpose each day. Remember, seeming roadblocks can be helpful redirects in disguise. No matter what is arising, you can know there are no mistakes; you are on a journey toward your own unfolding. All are learning experiences; there is no failure. Everything is given for your highest good and evolution. Above all, never give up; have faith and trust that all is unfolding in perfect timing.

Work in networks and partnerships with others who are dreaming a similar purpose. Your united intention and action will have a strong impact. Take purposeful action together. Use the intention of "we" rather than just "I." The power of coordinated action together creates your manifested goal more quickly and easily. As you shift your mentality from ownership and individual ego to sharing and working with others, so much more will be accomplished. The results will be miraculous as you work together for the higher good.

Part 3
Light Messages and Activations from Stella Maris

Embrace Child Power

Stella Maris Children Messengers:

Kaleosi, Luz, Lolli, Ra, Phaedra, and Ama

Who is the greatest in the kingdom of heaven?
And Jesus called a little child unto him, and set him in the midst of them,
And said, Verily I say unto you, except ye be converted, and become as little
children, ye shall not enter into the kingdom of heaven. (Matthew 18)

Stella Maris Children Speak:

We are the Stella Maris children. One of our most special missions is to be the guardians of children across the universe. Stella Maris was called by the Earth's children, to work as angelic guides who can intervene on their behalf. We are devoted to the well-being of all children, childhood, and your inner children.

The Stella Maris High Council is assisting with the unprecedented arrival of the Crystars and other light activator children. It is our greatest honor to serve in this way. We guide them from the higher realms to embodiment here on Earth. Starseed children will be the ones to ultimately heal this world. Honor them, for they hold the keys to a peaceful future and offer the gifts of vivid imagination, inspired awe, and joyful creation. Recognize them as great teachers of the possibility for human evolution. Please understand that physical age is an illusion and has no relationship to divine wisdom. The abilities that come naturally to children—imagination, joy, and creativity—are what is needed to steer this world out of crisis and into balance. Child power is the antidote for the world you are experiencing now.

If you are an adult, we invite you to embrace your inner children. Your phoenix child will return your precious abilities of imagination, joy, laughter, wonder, play, love, and light. Our messages, activations, and guided visionary journeys will help you heal all of your inner children and will activate the consciousness of your phoenix child. Restoring the link to the pure one within is key to your awakening and contribution to world healing. Our messages and guided meditations are also designed to support light activator children throughout their journey to adulthood.

Chapter 9
Kaleosi
Messenger of Divine Vision

Kaleosi Speaks:

I am Kaleosi, a one-year-old girl in the pod of Stella Maris. My name means "pure voice calling or inviting," and I am delighted to meet you. My pure voice reaches out to you beyond time and space so we can connect heart to heart. Honored to be the first Stella Maris messenger to communicate with you, I bless you with the gold ray to activate your visionary ability. This ray also awakens your memory of volunteering on Earth and reminds you of the important work we are here to do together.

Your heart is your guide for planetary changes to come, because its pure nature carries the resonance of love, magic, hope, and joy. Our joyous hearts will lead the great revolution of peace. Although I am chronologically young, I possess great wisdom. Remember to listen to the voices of the young, for they are strongly connected to the Divine Mother. I bring you messages of hope for your collective future and share my divine vision for Gaia Earth during our guided journey. My wish is to help you realize your true self, super powers, and innate gifts.

My Message for You: You Are a Volunteer

There is a great awakening underway on Earth, a movement that will restore balance and peace to this world. Do not become disheartened by the way the world appears, for there is a powerful and undetected healing movement underway. You may not hear about it on the news, but the Divine Mother is intervening on behalf of all life. You are here to witness the great awakening and revolution of unity consciousness. Wowza! Remember, you will activate the light and love that will create lasting peace. What a miraculous purpose!

All systems here will change, one awakening moment at a time. We will anchor and awaken new consciousness on Gaia Earth, and this awareness will change how human beings interact with the world around them. We will realign human evolution with divine principles.

You may have experienced the Earth as strange and unfriendly. The modern world can seem very brutal, because it is currently operating from a low level of consciousness. Love as an operating system has yet to take hold, and this is why you have come. You are a volunteer, a light activator who has come to help. You may have felt you didn't belong here, but the truth is you are a perfectly designed being of light, sent with an important mission. The term "light activator" describes all those light beings who have volunteered to help with this great change.

You do not need to fit into the world as it is. Instead, you are called to stand in the brightness of your divine light, and love it to awakening. You were born with visionary abilities and powers of the light. Should you choose to activate your powers, your presence will ignite a wave of love and light on Earth.

You are here to change everything for the better. Your existence here is more than wonderful! An angel on Earth, you are the one Gaia Earth has been waiting for. You were made for these times, a divine being in human form. Living your divinity will lead all beings out of the darkness. Your radiance will awaken and activate others to remember. It all starts with your willingness to heal yourself. Give yourself the gift of healing. Your life can become a living prayer for the healing of this world. Anchor yourself in the energy of the light through the vibrations of joy, happiness, and love. You are all transmitters of energy, and your being vibrates at certain frequencies as you send and receive energy every day, to and from everyone and everything around you. I invite you to cultivate your ability to rest in the light of your heart, where love and joy abound.

When you place your attention on suffering, problems, and violence, a dark energy is invited into your being, which you then unconsciously emit back into the world. It is sort of like eating really unhealthy food. It might seem exciting at first, but then you feel really sick. You are absorbing energy constantly, so be very careful about the vibratory energy you allow in your life through your choices, attention, and relationships.

Light activators often match the energy of others because of their great empathy, but you are being called to transcend this tendency by raising your vibration as a light activator. You can still help others, but in a different way. You are a light bringer, and your journey starts with your willingness to heal and activate your own light.

You Are a Visionary Imagineer

Hold the vision of the world you have come to create. Activate your light, beauty, creativity, and artistry to revolutionize our world. The more you live in alignment with your Higher Self and awaken your gifts, the quicker that positive changes will take hold. By embracing your purpose and the path of your heart, your inner joy will be ignited. Joy shifts consciousness easily.

Help me to find other light activators so they too can remember who they are and why they are here. Human light activators can be any age—babies, children, teens, or adults. There is no limitation due to chronological age, for age is truly an illusion. Let us create a community of connection and support for our work together.

We are here to be Imagineers who shape a bright future for all of life. We are the visionaries who can imagine the possible and engineer a new way of life. Gaia Earth's future depends on us. Together, we will create a divinely guided future. We will initiate a new golden era of peace, connection, balance, and love. My hopeful vision for our blessed future makes me leap for joy. Let's bless the Earth with our brilliant light. Together we will rise as one being.

Practices for Developing Your Visionary Ability

- Raise your frequency by inviting your Higher Self presence to guide your life.
- Choose to participate in activities that charge your energy and are in alignment with your highest divine service.
- Commit to shifting anything in your life that is no longer in alignment with your Higher Self and purpose. Set the intention to find other light activators.
- Walk the Beauty Way, living with the power of your light and love.
- Watch for signs and synchronicities, as your light activator tribe will begin to appear in your life. You can find them through causes or organizations devoted to things you are passionate about.
- Follow your bliss and make room in your life for the things that energize you.
- Set boundaries with people or activities that are no longer serving your highest good, making room for the new that will come.
- Use guided visualizations to develop the muscle of your inner sight and imagination.
- Engage in other practices that align you with your Higher Self, such as meditation and time in Nature.
- Remember who you are and why you are here.
- Embrace the sheer beauty and light of you, marvel at who is looking back at you in the mirror!
- Listen to the wisdom of children. They hold great powers of wonder, imagination, and renewal.
- Practice using your imagination to create the reality you choose to live in.
- Use the power of the spoken word and of your voice to affirm all your wishes for Earth and your life.
- Use the power of prayer to revolutionize your life. Prayer is focused intention; you are not necessarily praying to someone outside of yourself. Rather, you are returning to the oneness within you, and directing your prayers to Source.
- Regularly envision a peaceful, balanced, and happy Earth, where all of life is honored.
- Heal and empower your inner child so he or she can lead and guide your life.
- Connect with the color gold in daily life and read aloud the Scroll of Divine Vision to anchor your visionary ability.
- Regularly exercise to anchor high vibrational energy in your physical body.
- Eat foods that energize your body optimally.

Kaleosi Divine Visionary Journey

The Prayer of Stella Maris

Divine Maha Ocean Mother:

Hold me in your warm embrace,
Float me in your cosmic ocean of grace.
Refresh me with your "I AM" presence,
Bless my waters with divine light and self-realization.
Weightless and suspended in light,
Wave after wave of divine love flows through my multidimensional form.
Vitality, health, and renewal restores me to my true self.
Receiving the light of the Divine Feminine.
Receiving the light of the Divine Masculine.
Healing balance within and without.
All parts of myself deeply loved.
No sound or movement, resting in your Oneness,
Great Mother of All of Life,
I remember who I am.
A starlight being, a beautiful creation of stardust and divine water light.
Living Divinity.
Surrounded by my divine family, I imagine the possible for all of life.
Returning to oneness,
I bless myself.
I love myself.
I know myself.
I am free.
I am my true self forevermore.

Let us begin:

I take three deep breaths and bring my attention to my heart. I am instantly transformed into a dolphin. Gliding through the ocean water with ease, I delight in my hydrodynamic ability, leaping in and out of the sea. Kaleosi appears in the blue water in front of me. The golden sun is setting on the horizon, creating shades of orange and yellow. We swim toward the sunset and our bodies meld with the warmth of the golden colors.

From underwater, I notice a figure hovering nearby. She stands as if by magic on the water's surface. It is Mother Mary. She wears a translucent pearl robe, which billows in the light breeze. Her head is adorned with a golden crown and pink roses. She smiles, welcoming us by placing her hand gently on her sacred heart. Her loving presence fills my heart with the love of the Divine Mother. Kaleosi instantly begins leaping out of the water, twirling and jumping all around her. Mother Mary's face shines bright like a full moon, and she laughs at the little dolphin. White light radiates from the bottom of her feet. I hear her voice: "Would you like to join us for a journey?" "Yes," I reply. She kindly gazes at the stars twinkling, and suddenly we are being lifted from the water. We rise toward the starry night, picking up speed as we climb higher. Many constellations come into clear view as we enter the black night of space.

We hover in space above Earth. A young girl arrives, floating from the direction of Sirius. Her long blond hair shimmers and moves in waves around her face. Her glimmering eyes are sapphire-blue, and she wears a silver jumpsuit and cape. "I am Marianna Rose," she speaks telepathically to me. Mother Mary extends her arms, greeting Marianna with a warm and lasting hug. Kaleosi floats through the air, placing a light kiss on the girl's cheek. I now realize I am in my human form and extend my hand to greet her. The blue and green Gaia Earth slowly spins her beautiful body below us.

Marianna Rose directs my eyes to the east, and I see a mirror image of our star system and Earth. Blinking to make sure I'm not seeing double, I realize I am standing at a portal between two different realities. We glide across the threshold toward the alternate Earth reality. A pair of beautiful white wings appear on my back and I fly effortlessly through space, as if I have always known how. A feeling of exhilaration charges my body with sparkling energy. Kaleosi flies through the air too, just like she swims through the water. She twirls and plays. Marianna giggles, swooping and diving with her own wings. Mother Mary stands at the portal, awaiting our return, with one of her beautiful feet in each reality.

We enter the alternate Earth's atmosphere as skydivers, our bodies descending like arrows toward a target. I feel like a golden phoenix, wings pulled tight, with flames of golden light shooting out behind me. I slow down to take in the beauty of this parallel Gaia Earth. The oceans are glowing, clean and clear. The whales and dolphins swim in the clear water, balancing the ocean ley lines and the planetary grid. They happily sing their ocean songs. There are vast, untouched forests, and I breathe a sigh of relief, knowing the tree beings are alive and happy. The air is pure and clear, because of their unified breath. I witness how the Solstar light activators maintain a close relationship with human beings and are honored for their wisdom. The birds are flourishing; they fly overhead in bliss, migrating and keeping the balance of the skies. Flowers bloom and crystal caves shine.

We slowly approach a human city. The buildings are beautifully designed and made of translucent crystal material. There are natural landscapes of waterfalls, gardens, and trees. I observe the humans, who look happy and peaceful. They are living in connection and alignment with each other and the natural world. Everyone has a home, food, support, and a place within the community. Marianna tells me they live with freedom, liberty, and happiness, and there is deep connection among families, communities, and countries. Different countries come together to make important decisions in a united alliance for world peace.

Resources are shared, and there is enough for all beings to thrive. Power is created from electromagnetic energy, sun, and wind. The houses are made of the same renewable crystal, and vehicles are magnetically powered. Plant and animal beings are thriving in their lush and nourishing habitats. The Earth's waterways flow unobstructed.

A school appears, where children of all ages are learning. They are joyful as they create from their imagination. Communicating through telepathy, each child is deeply empathetic. I watch as one child manifests a crystal by harnessing the power of an orange flame. He holds it in the palm of his hand and the other children delight in his magical abilities. Their joy is contagious, and I giggle too. The school values cooperation, tolerance, and peace. Each child is regarded as a miracle in human form.

I smile at Mariana Rose and Kaleosi as they point toward a nearby home. Gazing below, I observe a mother holding her baby. Seeing the new precious life takes my breath away. How lucky for this baby to be born into this peaceful world! Don't all beings deserve this opportunity? The mother senses our presence and smiles. "Thank you," she says, "for all you are doing to secure this bright way of life for your world. We are forever grateful." A wave of joy flows through the top of my head, golden light pouring through my body. This alternate Earth has given me a glimpse of what is possible for Gaia Earth, and I am forever changed by the magnificent vision I have received.

Kaleosi motions that it is time to go. After taking one last look, I rocket into the starry sky. The wind flows through my hair, as I do a few hundred somersaults and cartwheels. We quickly approach Mother Mary where she is waiting. I land softly beside her, and she enfolds me in her dark blue cloak of stars. I am weightless, filled with divine love, the heart of the Great Divine Mother flowing through me.

Mother Mary speaks to me. "You are deeply loved, you are deeply held, you are deeply cherished, you are the beloved of my heart, you are my one and only divine creation, you are supported by thousands of beings, you are beautiful, you are strong, you are my heart walking around in the world. Don't forget, never forget. All you have witnessed is possible on Earth in your time. Do not lose hope. Imagine the possibilities. Remember this vision and bring it back to the world. Share it with others." I can no longer feel my body, as I melt into her love and rest in a quiet, noiseless space, beyond space and time. I am. I am. I am.

After some time, my eyes open to the shining face of Mother Mary. She slowly releases me from her embrace and removes a small bottle from her robe. She pours rose oil onto her fingers and presses it onto my third eye chakra, anointing me with the gift of divine vision. Deep indigo blue light flashes, as I receive this great blessing. "Your visionary ability is healed, and you can see clearly the divine vision for your Earth," Mother Mary whispers. I notice Mariana Rose is waiting to say goodbye. We hug, and I express my gratitude for her guidance on the visionary journey. She laughs and says, "You're welcome, sweetheart!" Kaleosi and I slowly descend to present-day Earth, gliding through the atmosphere and clouds. My feet land gently on the ground. Kaleosi is floating above me. She gently kisses my cheek and disappears. In my hand appears an ancient scroll. I open it and read aloud:

The Scroll of Divine Vision

Standing in the power and peace of my divinity, I proclaim:

I am a visionary

I am a divine messenger of light

My purpose is to hold a beautiful vision for Gaia's future

My visionary ability is fully restored, and I see eyes of divine sight

I create through the power of my imagination and guided action

I am an Imagineer of the new world

I clearly envision a future of balance and harmony

Uniting with others, I create unified fields for positive change

Anything is possible

In unity consciousness, I am guided by the Divine Mother

I return to oneness, the source of my divinely guided ideas

I am deeply loved

I deeply love

My inner child leads my way

I fly upon the wings of resurrection, a golden phoenix of light

Unity, peace, and balance is possible on Gaia Earth,
and I activate my abilities to make it so

And so it is

Chapter 10
Luz
Messenger of Divine Light

Luz Speaks:

I am Luz, messenger of divine light. My name means "pure light," and I bless you with the rose pink ray of healing. Appearing as a pink dolphin, I am very unique, and I offer you the gift of remembering the uniqueness of your own sacred heart light. Thank you for meeting me so we can delve into your infinite light together.

My Message for You

Have you ever felt like a dim candle, burning just enough to survive and not enough to thrive? I am here to charge your inner light with the pink ray. Your divine light burns forever bright at the center of your being. Some refer to this as the sacred heart, the light of your true identity. The fanning of your light creates a glow of brightness that can guide your life. Return to the oneness of your radiant light self and invoke your brilliance into daily life.

In your world, famous people are called stars. This is not an accident, for they are living creatively, stepping into their light and sharing their gifts. You are all stars in human form; that is why we refer to you as Starseeds. You possess unique gifts, and I encourage you to shine your light in different ways. Be willing to step into the light of your soul and radiate light in a thousand directions. This is what you are meant to do.

Once upon a time, there was a beautiful and rare white diamond. Its multifaceted surface shone with the light of a thousand stars. People traveled from far and wide to see this most precious gem. One day the diamond was sold, and needed to be moved to a new location. Many safety measures were put in place to protect the precious cargo during transport. The most successful diamond thief in the world heard about the diamond's transport and began planning how he would steal it.

He followed the museum curator with the diamond onto the train. He waited for his chance to steal the precious gem, but he could not find it. Never experiencing such failure, many feelings arose within his heart: despair, frustration, and finally curiosity. Approaching the museum curator, he announced, "I am the most successful diamond thief in the history of the world, yet I was unable to steal your diamond. I must know, what is your secret? Why was I unable to find it?"

The museum curator smiled, reached forward, and pulled the diamond out of the thief's own pocket. "Well, if you must know, I hid the diamond in the only place you would never look . . . on you." The beautiful diamond emerged, shining like a brilliant sun in the curator's hand. "Sometimes what you seek is already with you. Don't ever forget to look to yourself first." And with that, the curator disappeared into the night. (Gangaji Retreat, 2012)

Dearest friend . . . how often have you searched for the light outside of yourself in other people, situations, or things? You have looked for so long outside of yourself, believing you were lacking what you needed most. Are you tired of looking and not finding what you seek? I have great news! You simply have forgotten the light of who you are. The good news is, this light can never be lost.

I bless you with the remembrance of your one true divine light. You are a rare and precious diamond, a brilliant white light being of love. Your heart is waiting for you to remember; all you have to do is to say yes! The visionary journey I offer you now will spark and reignite your pink rose light so you can rest more effortlessly in your own divine nature. May you be delighted by the rediscovery of your divine light!

Practices to Activate Your Inner Light

- In the morning, hold your hand over your heart. Close your eyes and visualize a bright diamond shining at the center of your chest. The light of the diamond is white, pink, and gold. Watch as the light extends through your entire body and out to the space around you: your home, town, country, and the entire world.
- Spend time in solitude, light a candle, and call on the help of your guides and angels to brighten you from the inside. Ask to be shown any issues that need to be healed or old beliefs that are dampening your light. Find healing modalities that you like, to mend your light body.
- Use this affirmation: "I am a diamond, pure, brilliant heart. I reclaim the power of my inner light. I use my love and light to bring forth beauty, healing, and love to the world. I recognize the light within me and restore the memory of my true and Higher Self."
- Bring the pink ray into your life through food, environment, clothing, and sacred objects. Meditate with the color pink. Buy rose quartz and place it nearby or on your body. Discover how it brings light healing. Purchase an ankh to use for your sacred space and ceremony. The ankh is a symbol of your eternal light.
- Use the Scroll of Divine Light to affirm and strengthen your inner divine light.

Luz Initiation of Divine Light

The Prayer of Stella Maris

Divine Maha Ocean Mother:

Hold me in your warm embrace,
Float me in your cosmic ocean of grace.
Refresh me with your "I AM" presence,
Bless my waters with divine light and self-realization.
Weightless and suspended in light,
Wave after wave of divine love flows through my multidimensional form.
Vitality, health, and renewal restores me to my true self.
Receiving the light of the Divine Feminine.
Receiving the light of the Divine Masculine.
Healing balance within and without.
All parts of myself deeply loved.
No sound or movement, resting in your Oneness,
Great Mother of All of Life,
I remember who I am.
A starlight being, a beautiful creation of stardust and divine water light.
Living Divinity.
Surrounded by my divine family, I imagine the possible for all of life.
Returning to oneness,
I bless myself.
I love myself.
I know myself.
I am free.
I am my true self forevermore.

Let us begin:

I take three deep breaths and close my eyes. Mother Mary stands before me, wearing a beautiful, bright blue flowing robe, with hundreds of pink roses suspended in the air around her. I inhale the sweet scent of roses and myrrh. Rays of pink light shine on my body, and my skin soaks up the light like a healing balm. Mother Mary is wearing a rose quartz mala around her neck. She lifts it over her head and places it around my neck. As I look closely at the beads, I notice there is a golden ankh at the center of the necklace. She takes my hands in hers and asks me, "Are you ready?"

"Yes," I whisper.

Standing on the white-sand beach, I gaze out toward the turquoise sea. The sound of waves soothes my ears, and the sunlight warms my face. Digging my toes into the sand, the warm water tickles my toes. I wade in deeper, the water rising around my waist. Mother Mary has vanished.

A small figure approaches me from underwater, creating currents on the surface. A tiny pink dolphin emerges, with her head above the water. I am awestruck, because I have never seen a pink dolphin before. She is playing with a light pink stone, flipping it out of the water and then diving down to retrieve it. She looks at me curiously, rising to the surface once more and speaking softly, "I'm Luz; you can call me Lu." She has beautiful sapphire-blue eyes and a shining smile. She giggles, her voice high and lovely like a bell. I notice her sparkling white teeth and tongue.

"Would you like to join me for an adventure?" Lu asks. "Sure!" I answer, jumping into the deep, warm water. She circles around me and we play together. Following her into the deeper water, I mimic her movements. I am surprised by how effortlessly I can breathe underwater. We play chase, and I am really fast in the water. Looking down, I discover my arms and legs have disappeared, and in their place are flippers and fins. I am a dolphin once again! "Don't worry," Lu says. "You can change back whenever you like."

What fun! I leap out of the water and land on the ocean's surface with a belly flop crash. "Follow me," says Lu. We swim to the open ocean, where the water is a deep azure blue. We descend quickly, as an underwater temple comes into view. It is made of white stone, with arches and tall pillars. A multicolor seaweed garden accents the front with beautiful coral. A gold, weathered door graces the front of the temple, and I recognize the symbol of the Vesica Pisces carved on its surface, a pair of circles overlapping that form the sign of infinity. To my surprise, the door slowly starts to open, and we swim inside. I am immediately blinded by a gigantic bright crystal that sits in the center of the temple. The crystal is pure white and about fifty feet tall. It is oblong and glows brightly in all directions. The inner temple walls are made of gold which reflects the light, creating a golden energy within the room.

I realize I am in my human form again, breathing easily in the underwater temple. Luz asks me to sit down, motioning to a nearby seat at the perimeter. She holds the rose quartz stone on the back of her flipper and takes it toward the center crystal. Placing her smaller crystal next to the white one, she activates the pink crystal. It begins to glow, brighter and brighter. She returns to me and drops the crystal into my hand, motioning for me to hold it to my heart. Pressing the shining stone to my heart, I am filled with the all-consuming presence of love. The love flows through my entire body, infusing me with brilliant light. The brightness of the temple becomes blinding, and I can no longer keep my eyes open. I close them, feeling the light pervade my body, mind, and spirit. Luz touches my head, heart, hands, and feet with her rostrum (nose). Her touch activates more and more light within my form. The scent of rose and seawater wafts across the room.

My heart chakra expands, opening wide. A bright pink flame appears at the center of my chest, and I watch as it burns any darkness within my heart. Past grief and pain releases and leaves my body as black smoke. The smoke rises and dissolves in the light of the temple. I am healed by the power of light. My body shudders as it releases long-forgotten sadness and stored pain. I patiently experience the release of all emotional blockages that no longer serve me. The warmth of the light soothes me, making the process easier.

After my healing is complete, I gaze lovingly at the central crystal. It has changed from white to pink and is a brilliant rose star, shining in all directions. My inner starlight merges with the light of the crystal. Resting in pure joy and happiness, I shine beyond all form in pink heaven. I realize the pink crystal has disappeared from my hands, and in its place is a pink lotus flower. Puzzled, I look at Lu. She points to my heart. "It is now within you!" Placing my hands on my chest, I feel its presence, the seat of my greatest light power. I am so grateful for Lu and the divine light healing ceremony.

The light within the temple dims, signaling that it is time to go. We exit the temple as the door slowly closes behind us. Reaching the water's surface, I take a deep breath, noticing my reflection in the water. My human skin looks translucent and white; I am radiating my inner divine light in a new way!

"You are beautiful!" Luz says, as she twirls us through the water, belly to belly. I kiss her head and thank her for the journey. She laughs, and light bubbles flow out of her mouth. She says, "May the light of your soul shine brighter every day, may the love of your true self expand, may you be a beacon of light for others. Friends forever?" She laughs.

"Yes, friends forever," I respond.

We reach the shore, and as she swims away I wave goodbye and blow her kisses. The edges of my aura shimmer with pink and gold light.

Mother Mary appears to my left, and I witness the sacred fire burning within her heart. It appears as a single flame, emanating love light. She whispers that the rose quartz necklace is a gift from her heart to mine and it will help connect me to my sacred heart, the one flame of all creation. I thank her, bowing to her on my knees in reverence. Placing my hands on my heart, I feel the diamond light within me. A scroll appears in my pocket. I unroll it and read aloud:

The Scroll of Divine Light

Standing in the power and peace of my divinity, I proclaim:

Star light, star bright, First star I see tonight
I wish I may, I wish I might, Remember My Divine Light

I am the divine flame of creation

My heart is a diamond, shining brilliantly at the center of my soul

I am one with my sacred heart

I connect to my love light daily
and shine its radiance for the benefit of all beings

My light is a beautiful gift to the world

I am the pure light of love

I am a lighthouse

Through the power of my "I AM" light presence,
I help others to ignite their own lights

My light heals all of my being

Reclaiming my divine light,
I remove any barriers that have clouded my light in the past

Pure rose light connects me with the pink ray for my healing

I am relieved of any and all searches outside of myself; what a relief!

I am what I have been looking for

I rest in the divinity of my pure starlight

And so it is

Chapter 11
Lolli
Messenger of Divine Joy

Lolli Speaks:

I am Lolli, messenger of divine joy. My name means "victory and strength." I offer you the blessing of the yellow ray, a color that holds the energy of bliss, wonder, and happiness. Living with joy infuses your life with pure elation. Awe is one of my best friends; we play together often! Divine joy is always present when you connect with the Divine Mother, your Higher Self. When you live joyfully, amazing experiences will flow into your life with ease.

My Message for You

Joy always resides in your heart, and I am here to help you find it again. I invite you to remember your joyful inner child. He or she holds the keys to your feelings of wonder, awe, fresh sight, and joy—for children see the magic in life and find delight in the smallest of things. They have not become dulled by the conditioning of the world. No matter how old you are chronologically, your joyful inner child always rests in a spacious field of delight, to guide your new awareness.

As you grew older, you were taught to put away your "childlike" feelings and to be responsible. Boring! You became trapped within the thinking mind, spending most of your time in thought, not really being alive within your life. This chronic thinking habit cuts you off from your joy, leaving you lifeless and unhappy. Your culture indoctrinates you with constructs and beliefs that promote suffering, stagnancy, and unhappiness. Your life quickly becomes black-and-white, without the rainbows of color and zest of life.

When you look at the world with the eyes of joy, you will be enthralled by the wonder and mystery of life. How does a bird sing so beautifully? How do colors appear within the clouds? Why are there rainbows? How do butterflies drink nectar? Joy is the gateway to becoming enlivened and curious once again.

Would you like to reclaim your joy? Would you like to be free of past social conditioning? Would you like to remember the enjoyment that rests at the center of your heart? The joy of life itself? Yes! OK, then, I will help you. Come with me on the journey to where your inner child resides. Reconnect with this beautiful, joyful being that is within you.

Practices to Activate Joy

- Look at the world through the eyes of your joyful inner child. Notice the wonder and awe of the world. How mysterious! How amazing! How wonderful!
- Bring the color yellow into your life through food, clothing, crystals, and other ways. Eat yellow foods like lemons, bananas, and papaya. See how the color yellow activates joy.

- Spend ten to fifteen minutes sitting in the sun, absorbing the healing power of sunlight.
- Engage in practices to heal your inner child. Become a wonderful mother and father to this special one within.
- Practice right-brain creative activities like painting, drawing, singing, dancing, photography, or cooking, that activate your brain pathways for joy.
- Say the following: "Each day I expand in joy and wonder and inspire others to do the same."
- Read the Scroll of Divine Joy to anchor the vibration of joy in your life.

Lolli Divine Joy Activation

The Prayer of Stella Maris

Divine Maha Ocean Mother:

Hold me in your warm embrace,
Float me in your cosmic ocean of grace.
Refresh me with your "I AM" presence,
Bless my waters with divine light and self-realization.
Weightless and suspended in light,
Wave after wave of divine love flows through my multidimensional form.
Vitality, health, and renewal restores me to my true self.
Receiving the light of the Divine Feminine.
Receiving the light of the Divine Masculine.
Healing balance within and without.
All parts of myself deeply loved.
No sound or movement, resting in your Oneness,
Great Mother of All of Life,
I remember who I am.
A starlight being, a beautiful creation of stardust and divine water light.
Living Divinity.

Surrounded by my divine family, I imagine the possible for all of life.
Returning to oneness,
I bless myself.
I love myself.
I know myself.
I am free.
I am my true self forevermore.

Let us begin:

I place my hand on my heart and take three deep breaths. A beautiful white-sand beach appears before me, and I am standing at the edge of the aqua water, full of excitement. I excitedly await my next light messenger. Listening to the sound of the waves, I relax more deeply to the whisper sound of ebb and flow. Flocks of birds glide over the water in perfect unity. The ocean water ripples—someone is coming. A small dolphin rises out of the water about ten feet in front of me, her tail propelling her small body above the surface. "I'm Lolli, messenger of divine joy. Would you like to join me for an adventure?"

"Yes," I reply.

Lolli swims closer, and as she reaches the beach she magically transforms into an eight-year-old girl. She has bright blond hair and violet eyes. She wears a simple white sari; her feet are adorned with turquoise blue jewels that are fastened around her ankles. She emerges from the water and begins to walk toward the jungle, motioning for me to follow. A winding path is revealed through the palm trees. As we enter the rainforest, the scent of damp earth and fresh rain infuse the air, and we continue to walk deeper and deeper into the jungle. Beautiful trees of every shape and color create a canopy of green light over our heads. Some are ancient, their gnarled bark showing faces of grandmothers and grandfathers. The trees grow together, creating a natural arch over our path. A feeling of wildness flows over me; I am not afraid to feel my freedom. I am at home here, knowing we are safe in the dark wild of the forest.

We reach a tall wooden doorway decorated with a half dome circle and surrounded in moss. Lolli knocks on the door three times, and it opens with a grinding creak. Entering the most beautiful clearing, I see an open meadow with flowing fields of wildflowers—white, purple, pink, orange, and yellow. Hundreds of butterflies fly among the flowers, their movements creating a swirling dance. Around the outer circle of the meadow stand tall, ancient trees—grandmother and grandfather Redwood trees—ancient beings who have guided us for eons with their wisdom. They smile at me, their bark revealing faces moving and alive. The garden has a large aquamarine pond in its center, with a hundred-foot-tall yellow lotus flower. The clouds above reflect the bright yellow light that shines from its stamen.

A child approaches us, walking with a magnificent white unicorn. My mouth drops open as I take in the beauty of a real unicorn and the presence of this radiant child. Instantly, I recognize that this is my joyful inner child. This is the place where she/he resides in safety and bliss. My joyful inner child walks carefully toward me, welcoming me to the garden. I wonder if I can touch the unicorn, and without me saying a word, the great white horse bows his head before me. I run my fingers through his pure, silky white hair. "Would you like a ride?" asks my joyful inner child. "I would love to," I respond. I am lifted by an unseen force and placed carefully on the back of the unicorn. Sinking my hands into his white mane, I hold on tight. The unicorn walks, trots, and then gallops, lifting us into the air above the garden. I ride with ease and perfect balance. My stomach churns with sheer excitement, and I laugh out loud with joy. We fly in circles, gliding up and down, fast and slow. The butterflies join us in our crazy dance, brushing my face and arms with their soft wings. The unicorn lands softly within the lotus and I slide off his back, my feet landing on the yellow stamens.

Surrounded by huge yellow petals, I gaze at the yellow light of the lotus, shining with diamond brilliance. The unicorn invites me to play a game. "Look for a yellow diamond," he says gently. I look down, noticing many shapes and sizes of yellow crystals under my feet. A yellow diamond heart appears, and I hold it softly in my hands. My inner child and Lolli appear next to me instantly. "This yellow ray diamond is our gift to you. It is a power object that will help you access your joyful heart wherever you go. You will never lose the connection to joy again," my joyful child says sweetly. She extends her hand toward me, and I gently place the diamond into her palm. She whispers a blessing into the diamond, kisses it, and then places it firmly against my solar plexus.

The power of joy shines through the center of my being. Waves of yellow and gold light fill me with feelings of elation and wonder. Closing my eyes, I receive this divine gift from Lolli and my joyful child. I open my eyes, seeing the yellow heart diamond merging with my body, dissolving and disappearing into my form. "It will always be with you," my inner child says.

The three of us hold hands, standing together at the center of the flower. The clouds above us are filled with multicolored rainbows and butterflies dancing in joyful spirals. The unicorn returns to my side and I hug him strongly, wrapping my arms tightly around his neck. We are lifted in the air together and land back in the garden. I hug my joyful child, Lolli, and then stroke the neck of my new unicorn friend. He nickers at me in recognition. I know it is time to go, and tears well up in my eyes. I will miss this beautiful garden of joy. We make our way back to the entrance. Taking one last look at the sheer beauty, Lolli approaches me and asks, "How did you like visiting the garden of en-joy-ment?" I laugh in response. "Very much indeed."

"Good news! You can return whenever you like!"

We walk back down the path through the forest and arrive on the beach. Lolli transforms into her dolphin form by diving gracefully into the sea. "Thank you," I shout. "I am so grateful for your blessings."

"You're welcome!" she replies from the water. "Until our joyful hearts meet again, my dear friend!" Her form disappears in the water. A scroll appears in my hand. I unroll it and read aloud:

The Scroll of Divine Joy

Standing in the power and peace of my divinity, I proclaim:

The gentle essence of my joyful heart sets my power in motion

Joy always rests at the center of my soul

When I am in joy I am connected to the Source

I am filled with the bright yellow ray light of joy

My inner joyful child holds the keys to my wonder

My inner joyful child experiences permanent healing now

Joy and radiance are my birthright

I am in awe of the beauty of life

I delight in my experiences

I jump for joy

Jump, Jump, Jump!

I reactivate my brain pathways to experience more joy

Joy runs from the tips of my toes to the top of my head

Joy tickles my soul, and I fall into a fit of laughter

A butterfly of joy rests in my solar plexus

The yellow ray and crystal permeate my being with lasting joy

I am wonder . . . I am joy . . . I am free

I am enchanted . . . I am in awe

And so it is

Chapter 12

Ra

Messenger of Divine Play

Ra Speaks:

I am Ra, messenger of divine play. My name means "the bright sun." I bless you with the radiance of the orange ray and the liberating power of play! Play gives you access to your highest intelligence and sparks your creativity. An essential activity for all beings, playful games bring Stella Maris together regularly—even the elders of our pod. We rock it with fun games and imaginings. Play is intrinsically linked to your imagination, magic, and creativity.

My Message for You

Unfortunately, in modern times you are taught that "growing up" means you can no longer play. In your culture, play is considered a childish waste of time, even when you are still children! What a farce! What a trap! Nothing could be further from the truth. A life without play is quite boring, and devoid of fun. I invite you to make play an important part of your life. You may worry that you have forgotten how to play, but your inner children have not. To restore your ability to play, you first need to re-connect with your inner phoenix child and invite him or her back into your life on a daily basis. This one within will bring you play, laughter, joy, and fun. Curiosity and adventure will return to your life as you embrace this new way of being.

Could you use more health, vitality, and happiness? All are increased by play! YES, please!!!!! Play lights up your neural pathways, creating a symphony of light and new connections within your brain. It brings delight and joy to your heart, cre-ating health and happiness in its wake. Play brings you vitality, optimism, and joy! YES, please!!!! The possibility of play exists in every present moment. Play allows you to step off the wheel of human-created time and to anchor more fully in the present moment. Time does not exist when you are playing, my friend, even when your entire culture is designed around this fake construct. I am Ra, master of play and liberator of time. I will help you engage in play, fully alive and free, existing in the domain of timelessness. Would you like to join me? Play today and do not delay!

Practices to Activate Divine Play

- Find the silly fun in your daily activities.
- Play games with others. Be willing to learn new ones and be open to different experiences.
- Connect and play with a child—they are excellent teachers of how to play.
- Practice being lighthearted. Do not let your serious self take over.
- Animals are also master teachers of how to play—observe and repeat! Visit the dolphins!

- Set the intention for more play to flow into your life, and watch what happens.
- Invite the orange color ray into your life. Eat orange fruit like oranges, carrots, and sweet potatoes. Wear orange, buy orange flowers or crystals. Meditate upon the color orange.
- Invoke the power of the Scroll of Divine Play by reading it aloud or using it as an affirmation daily.
- Ask your Higher Self for help with playing. Find opportunities and ways to play, for it is a remembered skill that comes with practice.

Ra Activation of Divine Play

The Prayer of Stella Maris

Divine Maha Ocean Mother:

Hold me in your warm embrace,
Float me in your cosmic ocean of grace.
Refresh me with your "I AM" presence,
Bless my waters with divine light and self-realization.
Weightless and suspended in light,
Wave after wave of divine love flows through my multidimensional form.
Vitality, health, and renewal restores me to my true self.
Receiving the light of the Divine Feminine.
Receiving the light of the Divine Masculine.
Healing balance within and without.
All parts of myself deeply loved.
No sound or movement, resting in your Oneness,
Great Mother of All of Life,
I remember who I am.
A starlight being, a beautiful creation of stardust and divine water light.
Living Divinity.
Surrounded by my divine family, I imagine the possible for all of life.

Stella Maris Speaks

Returning to oneness,
I bless myself.
I love myself.
I know myself.
I am free.
I am my true self forevermore.

Let us begin:

I place my hand on my heart and take three deep breaths. I am floating on my back, gazing at the expansive blue sky. Soothing water flows around me, bubbles tickle my body as they float up from below. Stella Maris is here, somewhere in the depths of the ocean underneath me. The sound of their sonar rises in the form of clicks, whistles, and dolphin songs. My body receives blessings from their sonar language of light. With my inner vision, I watch symbols of light and sacred geometric shapes dissolve on my skin. The symbols activate and heal my consciousness.

Stella Maris comes closer, rising in a V-formation from the bottom of the sea. Something tickles my feet, and I see a small dolphin with a beaded orange necklace.

"I am Ra, lover of life, and master of play! Would you like to play?"

"Yes!" I answer. As Ra dives deep I follow, easily transforming into my dolphin form. I am greeted by the entire pod of Stella Maris and quickly realize this will be a group game. We swim together toward the ocean floor and arrive at a most beautiful coral reef. The reef is full of vibrant fish. The coral glows with otherworldly light and has an abundance of bright orange crystal formations. The crystals cast a warm, golden-orange light on the sea floor.

Ra separates our teams and explains the rules of the game—an underwater Stella Maris version of capture the flag. A green piece of seaweed will be our flag, and the other team's is bright red. Each team places their seaweed in a secure location, and the game begins. Telepathically, we create a plan for capturing the other team's seaweed. Ra and I will be the seaweed finders. We glide around rocks, sneaking and hiding, the excitement churning my stomach. Quiet as can be, we approach the red seaweed that is guarded by Lolli. Ra swims one way to distract her and I swim the other way, quickly grabbing the flag and bursting back to our side. We win!!! Elation and joy fills me; what fun! Our team leaps together in unison above the water's surface.

Ra motions for me to follow him back to the sea floor. He places a large orange crystal pendant around my neck. "Keep this, so you will always remember the fun of play!" he says kindly. "You are always invited to play with us!" The entire pod has returned, creating a symphony of sonar and dolphin clicks. The light of the orange ocean crystals merges with my tangerine-colored pendant. I fully receive the blessing of divine play. Oceanic beings arrive all around us—manta rays, whales, turtles, and fish. Swirling around me, they bless me, play, and demonstrate our transcendent connection.

I thank Stella Maris and the ocean beings for the game and all of their gifts. Ra and I swim to the surface and arrive at the white-sand beach. He spins through the air, waving goodbye. "Play, play every day!" he shouts. A scroll floats toward me. I unroll it and read aloud:

The Scroll of Divine Play

Standing in the power and peace of my divinity, I proclaim:

Play is my way

Play activates my highest intelligence
and creates new energetic pathways on all levels of my being

I make time to play every day

Embracing play as a way of life, I invite others to join me
through my lighthearted laughter and joy

Play frees me from the restraints of human-created time

I am free in the now of every moment

Play is vital to my health and well-being

New adventures and experiences give me opportunities to play more

I reclaim the power of my inner child, who can show me how to play

My playful inner child delights in my beautiful life

I create new ways to play

Playing each day keeps the doctor away

I am living a juicy, play-filled life

I find friends to play with

I reclaim the power of my playful heart

And so it is

Chapter 13
Phaedra
Messenger of Divine Laughter

Phaedra Speaks:

I am Phaedra, messenger of divine laughter. My name means "bright one," and I bless you with the radiance of the violet ray, which activates your sense of humor. Laughter is an incredible healing practice!

My Message for You

In the book *Peter Pan*, it is said that when the first baby laughed, the laughter spread into a thousand sparks of light. This light gave birth to magical fairies. Divine laughter truly does create this kind of magic and can transcend any seeming limitation instantly. Laughter is one of your greatest gifts from the Divine Mother, an audible expression of joy. If you could see the energy of laughter, it would look like shimmering, colorful balls of light floating all around you; laughing orbs!

Laughter can realign the energy of your physical body, allowing it to flow freely. Giggles, just like yawns, are contagious, spreading seeds of joy and happiness upon the wind. Being around others who are lighthearted raises your vibration. When was the last time you laughed? A really good laugh? One that makes you cry, snort, and bellyache?

Spend time each day laughing. Just like you meditate or practice yoga, devote time to laughter. Find things that are amusing to you! You can look up videos of babies and dolphins laughing on YouTube or watch comedy on your TV. Baby laughter is the best, I tell you. Human babies laugh at two months old, before they can walk or talk. Laughter is their first language, a perfect expression of their inner light. Renew your spirit and bring ease to your soul through the power of laughter. It renews your life force and gives you a fresh perspective. Laugh today and every day!

Practices for Activating Divine Laughter

- Watch funny movies, YouTube videos, or TV shows. Go to a comedy event.
- Find ways to add silly and a dash of crazy into your life.
- Attend a laughter therapy group. Do intentional laughing. Start with a fake laugh—it can build into real laughing, especially when you laugh in a group.
- Be creative with your sense of humor.
- Smile more often and find the humor in your everyday life. See the ridiculousness of the world, and instead of becoming upset, laugh!
- Connect with the violet color ray through crystals, clothing, environment, and food. This color will bring more laughter to you. If you activate your joy and play, laughter won't be far behind.
- Use the Scroll of Divine Laughter as an affirmation or intention for activating more laughter in your life.
- Again, follow the lead of your inner joyful child. She or he knows how to find the funny in every situation.

Phaedra Activation of Divine Laughter

The Prayer of Stella Maris

Divine Maha Ocean Mother:

Hold me in your warm embrace,
Float me in your cosmic ocean of grace.
Refresh me with your "I AM" presence,
Bless my waters with divine light and self-realization.
Weightless and suspended in light,
Wave after wave of divine love flows through my multidimensional form.
Vitality, health, and renewal restores me to my true self.
Receiving the light of the Divine Feminine.
Receiving the light of the Divine Masculine.
Healing balance within and without.
All parts of myself deeply loved.
No sound or movement, resting in your Oneness,
Great Mother of All of Life,
I remember who I am.
A starlight being, a beautiful creation of stardust and divine water light.
Living Divinity.
Surrounded by my divine family, I imagine the possible for all of life.
Returning to oneness,
I bless myself.
I love myself.
I know myself.
I am free.
I am my true self forevermore.

Stella Maris Speaks

Let us begin:

I place my hand on my heart and take three deep breaths. I am floating on my back in the middle of a purple sea. Theseus appears above my head. To my left are Mahadra and Kaleosi, to my right are the dolphin children, Lu, Ra, Ama, Lolli, and Phae, and at my feet are Grandmother Izoma, Grandfather Skylan, Kelti, and Drahana. They swim in a circle, creating a vortex of spinning water around me. I quickly shape-shift into my dolphin form and join them. We swim in grand circles, stirring the energy of the Ocean Mother. As we leap together to the water's surface I begin to laugh uncontrollably from the thrill.

A small dolphin with light blue eyes invites me to follow her. We enter a dark tunnel, swimming in pure blackness for what seems like forever. Finally a glowing light appears, and we surface near a pristine island.

The sound of high and beautiful voices meets my ears. They are singing and laughing. Colored balls of light flutter close; the auras of tiny winged fairies. The fairies are dancing in the wind as Phae calls them close. We are surrounded by fairies of every color. They introduce themselves one by one, sharing their names and laughing uncontrollably. Their laughter sounds like small, resonant bells, each with a slightly different tone.

I shift back into my human form as I walk onto the beach. The fairies fly all around me, chatting, smiling, and laughing. A small violet fairy sits in my hand, directing me to walk toward a deep woodland forest. The forest is green and lush, with the sound of a nearby stream. The forest path reveals every flower the world has ever known. The fairy explains that this is a source island where all of the plants, trees, and flowers that have ever been or will ever be are cultivated. I observe how each flower is tended by many guardians, including the Nature devas, bees, and the lady bugs. She tells me how every flower is the result of an enlightened plant. Plants can awaken to their spiritual oneness and bloom into flowers through their awakening. I gaze at the Nature devas, the overlighting being of each plant. They are beautiful as they move around the flowers; sometimes invisible, sometimes appearing in shapes and colors.

We arrive at a large orange-and-pink cushion leaning against a tall tree, and the fairies invite me to sit. The fairies create a circle around me, as a young girl with brown hair and beautiful blue eyes approaches. She is about ten years old. She winks at me, and I realize it is Phae in her human form!

Phae is wearing a flowing violet dress embroidered with seashells, with white flowers braided throughout her long hair. She sits across from me and the fairies begin to sing in harmonizing tones. Sparkling gold fairy dust drifts toward me, brushing against my cheek and body. It tickles my nose, and I sneeze! The intoxication of the gold dust makes me want to laugh. I try to contain it, but then it grows into a belly-shaking, nose-snorting, eyes-tearing laugh. My stomach hurts, and I feel like I may explode with joy. Phae is laughing too, and she rolls back in a fit of uncontrollable giggles. Tears are streaming down my face, my tongue is salty, and my belly shakes. My laughter rises as balls of colored light, floating around the island like balloons. The fairies laugh with us, and we just can't stop.

My laughter lifts me off the cushion, and I dance in the air, with fairies all around. My body moves rhythmically to the beat of my inner joy. I spin in circles and join hands with Phae, who is floating nearby. The fairies sprinkle us with more golden dust, and we float higher and higher above the ground. My inner child remembers how fairy dust and happy thoughts can make you fly. I realize it is true! I am flying!

I swoop through the forest, flying low over the flowers and trees. Following the river, I fly with butterflies, who swirl with me in creative shapes. Exhausted, I land under a palm tree, returning to my human form. The forest is quiet, still, and peaceful. The scent of flowers calms my spirit. A fairy dressed in bright pink and orange lands next to me, handing me a small cluster of violet crystals. I receive her gift in the palm of my hand.

"This is the gift of laughter," she says. "Don't forget, it is always with you. The crystals of laughter will restore your humor."

Thanking her with a smile, I look closely at the purple crystals that glow with an otherworldly hue.

"It is time to return," Phae says. I am startled by instantaneous hugs from hundreds of little bodies, and I laugh once more. We walk to the water's edge as I wave goodbye to the fairies who have gathered in small circles. Diving into the water, we journey back through the tunnel and the open ocean. I wave goodbye to Phae, thanking her for our journey together. I wade out of the seawater and stand on the white-sand beach. I discover a scroll tucked into my pocket. I open it and read aloud:

The Scroll of Divine Laughter

Standing in the power and peace of my divinity, I proclaim:

My laughter emanates the high vibrations of joy and light

My lighthearted laughter sets my power into motion

The golden dust of delight infuses every cell of my body with elation

Laughter is one of the greatest medicines for my soul

No darkness can withstand the presence of laughter

My laughter blesses all of life through its magical tones of happiness

I embrace my laughter daily, knowing it has healing power

I laugh often and deeply

My funny bone is mended, and I exercise it regularly

I call forth my inner child, who remembers how to snort and giggle

My laughter sends waves of happiness throughout my body

My belly shakes like a bowl full of jelly

My eyes water with tears of joy

I hold the violet crystals with me always, the keys of laughter

I remember how good-feeling thoughts allow me to fly freely

I reclaim my laughter and joy

And so it is

Chapter 14

Ama

Messenger of Divine Love

Ama Speaks:

I am Ama, messenger of divine love. My name means "heavenly water," and I bless you with a rainbow ray of everlasting love. My presence activates the serenity of your heart chakra and Higher Self. I am a white dolphin, and my pure color actually holds the entire spectrum of all colors, as they fuse together into white light. My nickname is rainbow girl.

My Message for You

Love is the universal energy wherein all positive energies exist. Love holds hope, kindness, faith, joy, laughter, compassion, trust, play, and light. Love is the primordial energy of existence itself and flows like a vast ocean within and all around you. Take a deep breath, resting your attention at your heart. Feel the waves of loving support that are available to you in every moment. Love is truly all there is, existing as the source of all healing. May all of your experiences arise out of the great love that you are.

I bless you with self-love, hope, and unlimited faith in the unfolding of your life. May you trust your heart, knowing that there is a greater divine plan in action. By aligning with the high vibration of love, may you experience more and more positive energies in your life. Know that everything will be OK and that you are a beloved one of Source. May you show up to your life with the trust and faith that only love can command. Experience how the Divine Mother rises up to support you when you are willing to receive her love.

Love is vulnerable, and your tender heart can be your greatest strength. Be vulnerable with others by showing your true self and speaking your truth. Find opportunities to practice self-love in ever-deepening measure. A self-love practice is the first step to your awakened life. Love your body as a living temple for your divine soul. Love yourself as the one divine heart. Give understanding and acceptance to all of your inner selves. Meet them with great love and compassion. Fall in love with your precious winged heart, for it is beautiful beyond measure. Extend your divine love to all beings, knowing their true identity of the one light. Time on Earth is precious, so tell your loved ones how you feel. Send your love to Gaia Earth and to all of life, for the energy of love is your greatest healing power.

Practices to Activate Divine Love

- Deepen your capacity for self-love through practices that honor you. Feed your body healthy food, rest, make sure you get enough sleep, adorn yourself in beautiful jewelry and clothes, choose to surround yourself with the people and activities that speak to your heart and energize you.
- Connect with the rainbow ray. Place rainbows in your sacred space through crystals, art, or other items.
- Imagine love as the greatest force in the universe, and visualize love permeating your being and flowing out to all beings.
- Connect with the presence of the Divine Mother, feeling the incredible love

offered to you from this source at any moment.

- Study light language and ancient symbols to bring into your daily life, to activate your divine love and Higher Self.
- Practice extending divine love to those who are closest to you. Be their soft place to fall. Wrap your arms around them with compassion and yourself.
- Use the Scroll of Divine Love to heal your heart.
- Practice being vulnerable and real in the world. This is the way of the divine feminine.

Ama Activation of Divine Love

The Prayer of Stella Maris

Divine Maha Ocean Mother:

Hold me in your warm embrace,
Float me in your cosmic ocean of grace.
Refresh me with your "I AM" presence,
Bless my waters with divine light and self-realization.
Weightless and suspended in light,
Wave after wave of divine love flows through my multidimensional form.
Vitality, health, and renewal restores me to my true self.
Receiving the light of the Divine Feminine.
Receiving the light of the Divine Masculine.
Healing balance within and without.
All parts of myself deeply loved.
No sound or movement, resting in your Oneness,
Great Mother of All of Life,
I remember who I am.
A starlight being, a beautiful creation of stardust and divine water light.
Living Divinity.
Surrounded by my divine family, I imagine the possible for all of life.

Stella Maris Speaks

Returning to oneness,
I bless myself.
I love myself.
I know myself.
I am free.
I am my true self forevermore.

Let us begin:

I place my hand on my heart and take three deep breaths. I am seated inside a glass temple with six equal sides and a dome roof. It stands by the sea next to a rocky beach and facing the ocean. Legs crossed and spine straight, I relax on a white meditation cushion while gazing at the aqua water. A gentle breeze invigorates my body as I breathe slowly in and out. The temple doors are open and the wind blows the sheer white drapes into beautiful forms.

The sun rises in the east, casting golden rays on the surface of the water. I feel my absolute oneness with all of creation. Gazing at my chest, I notice a round white diamond pendant around my neck. The morning light shines throughout the temple and reflects in my pendant, radiating colorful rainbows in every direction. I laugh out loud with delight that I finally found the end of a rainbow!

Someone is calling my name from the sea. Rising slowly, I stretch my hands above and bring them to my heart. I slip on white shoes and carefully walk down the rocks to the ocean's edge. Before me is a most beautiful white dolphin. She swims back and forth, playing along the shore, and stops directly in front of me. She introduces herself telepathically as Ama and invites me on a journey. I accept and dive into the clear aqua water beside her, immediately transformed into my dolphin form, which is familiar and natural.

Ama's white body casts a beautiful glow under the water, as her white light shines like a star. Beyond, the white light rainbow aura reflects upon the white sand. We play and swim together, enjoying each other's company and the touch of the seawater. She motions for me to follow her to the depths below.

An underwater temple appears: a golden dome, rising in intricate Moroccan patterns. It has high pillars and an arched double door. The temple doors open in unison as we enter. My eyes take in the courtyard, planted with flowering water plants and gold fish. We enter the temple with reverence. The presence of divine love pervades the entire space. My necklace glows brightly here, as I shift back into my human form. Ama leads me around the outer temple, and we stop at six different gold columns. There is one column in each corner of the temple, each with sacred geometric symbols and jewels. We offer a sea flower to each pillar and then walk along the outer temple wall. The walls are also made out of gold, with many sections inscribed with light language. Running my hand along the carved symbols, I wonder what wisdom they are holding. The thought crosses my mind that this could be the Akashic records.

Ama invites me to join her inside the inner temple. A two-hundred-foot glowing white crystal sits at the center. Surrounding the central crystal are crystals of different colors: blue, purple, green, orange, yellow, and red, each glowing brightly.

A ceremony is beginning. The room becomes completely dark, and I watch as the red crystal begins to glow, filling the room with a ruby light essence. I turn my palms up, watching in astonishment as the red light enters the center of my hands and the soles of my feet. The red light slowly fades as the orange crystal becomes bright, filling the room with tangerine light. The light shines upon my body, lingering near my sacral chakra and nose. The orange light slowly fades as the yellow crystal glows, filling the room with sunny yellow light, which enters my solar plexus and head. After the yellow slowly fades, the green crystal glows, emerald entering my heart. I notice how Ama's body changes with each new color ray, her white form a perfect reflective surface. The blue crystal shines brightly, flowing through every color on the blue spectrum. It casts blue light on my throat chakra and third eye, and later the purple and indigo rays shine through the top of my head. Finally, all of the colors shine together and dissolve into one white light. The intensity of light forces me to close my eyes, and with my inner sight I witness each of my chakras spinning in unison, creating their own spirals. White light from above descends into my body. As the rays flow through my body, there is an immediate release of old thoughts, beliefs, and self-judgment. I witness how they are transmuted by love. Sometimes old sufferings appear in diverse shades of gray or black. They resist the light at first, but then surrender as they dissolve in the arms of the light. Taking a deep breath, I wrap my arms around my body, hugging myself tightly. I feel how intensely I love myself. My form dissolves into the white light, pervaded by love. I remember and know myself. Here I rest, weightless and formless.

After some time, I open my eyes. Ama floats in front of me, smiling brightly. She tells me it is time to return, and we exit the inner sanctuary. As we pass through the outer temple, I realize that I can read and understand all of the symbols carved on the walls. Something has shifted, and I now understand the ancient light language. Ama explains that I can return any time to study the teachings within the temple. She tells me how the wisdom is inscribed with light language, a primordial language created by the Divine Mother. The Higher Self of all beings can understand it easily. She shares with me that light language is a highly evolved communication tool that combines physics, sacred geometry, sound, and light.

As we exit, I bow to the sacred gold temple with gratitude. I swim through the open ocean, taking my dolphin form once again. When I arrive at the glass temple, it is night. The stars in the night sky shine brightly, especially the constellation of the Pleiades. I imagine the seven sisters winking at me and sparkling messages of love. A shooting star blazes over my head, leaving a bright trail in its wake. Ama and I jump for joy in the sea as more shooting stars zoom above us, creating a brilliant light show. Then it is quiet and dark. I express my gratitude to Ama, hugging her, belly to belly. My human form slowly returns, and I leave the water. I notice a scroll in my hand. The glass temple is glowing in front of me, illuminated by thousands of white candles. I open the scroll and read aloud:

The Scroll of Divine Love

Standing in the power and peace of my divinity, I proclaim:

I am love, I am the one true heart

My crystalline heart shines with the white brilliance of a thousand colors

My winged heart is precious and stands strong in its vulnerability

Love is who I am and all there is

Love is the primary energy of joy, light, laughter, trust, faith, play, and hope

Where there is love there is light

My heart shines with rainbow healing and the white ray of freedom

I am a rainbow, I am a shooting star

My heart has wings

Within my vulnerability, my strength lies

I love fully and freely

I extend the love that I am to all beings

I am love and compassion

My sacred heart has wings

Love is the primordial force of the universe

Love is the force that moves the Earth and stars

Love heals all, Love is kind, Love is real, Love is trust

Love is the greatest power of the universe

And so it is

Stella Maris Adult Messengers and Queen A'Mara: Theseus, Mahadra, Grandmother Izoma and Grandfather Skylan, Kelti, and Drahana

Stella Maris Speaks:

The second group of Stella Maris light messengers is the teen and adult members. In the next chapters, we will offer guidance, activations, and blessings to help you rediscover your ancient wisdom. We will share about connecting with water as a healing medium, restoring your human senses, and activating your quantum abilities. Stella Maris and Queen A'Mara speak of how to live in alignment, create space for your emotions, and grace you with the knowledge of your nobility. Our messages, journeys, and activations will assist your awakening beyond measure! Enjoy the next round of messages and guided visionary meditations, as you dive in with our great wise ones.

Chapter 15

Theseus

Messenger of Ancient Wisdom

Theseus Speaks:

I am Theseus, a wise elder in the pod of Stella Maris. My Greek name means "hero," "man of action," and "unifying king." I use this name to signify my role as leader of a peaceful revolution on Earth. I carry the wisdom of the ages and participate on the council of Stella Maris as a philosopher, mystic, scholar, and teacher. I bless you with the silver ray of eternal wisdom. As a living embodiment of the divine masculine, I am Stella Maris's light-language historian and story keeper. I keep records of Earth history and have experienced many incarnations in both human and dolphin form. I will share some of the stories from my lifetimes on Earth, especially in ancient Greece, in hopes it will help you remember your own. Through the power of memory, you can recover your divine knowledge and eternal wisdom.

My Message for You

You are a light activator who will ignite the divine revolution of peace. Through the power of your wisdom, old structures and social conditioning will dissolve and be replaced by new ones. You are the key to this awakening. The only way to heal the darkness on Earth is through the power of love.

The first step in healing is your personal divine remembrance. You are a master light worker with many selves who have trained for eons in the sacred arts, healing, and spirituality. I invite you to remember your divinity and ancient wisdom. The second step is to release outdated beliefs and thoughts that you have been indoctrinated with in your modern-day culture. This will free you and allow you to embody your Higher Self to a higher degree. Remember, your ancient Higher Self is eternal and transcends time and space. You carry all the wisdom you will ever need within. Know thyself and remember who you really are. "Να θυμάσαι ποιος είσαι."

My Story

Theseus Speaks:

Each of my lifetimes was a conscious choice. My home star system is the Pleiades and where I exist in my light-body angelic form. I am the third son in a family with seventeen children. My mother is a star priestess and my father is a social leader and visionary. As a being of light, I can appear however I like, often appearing as waves of color and light.

My early existence in the Pleiades was filled with joy, connection, and creativity. I attended school, learning record and story tending from my elders. Once I completed my training, I was invited to offer my service through travel to other planets and star systems. The beautiful Gaia Earth enamored me, and I decided to volunteer to help with her planetary evolution. Because of this commitment, I participated in many lifetimes on Earth.

On the day I left for my first Earth mission, my mother and father took me in their arms and blessed me. They told me they were proud of who I was and that they knew I would help many beings. My mother cried as I kissed her cheeks to say goodbye. She understood the gravity of my mission and that I was consenting to experience the danger and suffering of life on Earth. The next morning, I departed with a large group of other light activators, journeying together into the unknown. We leapt into the starry night, leaving behind us a trail of white stardust. We floated above Gaia Earth's atmosphere, carefully selecting our first life experience. The first form I chose was that of a dolphin. I spoke my intention aloud, and all sound ceased. I was weightless and formless. Slowly, I became aware of floating in the watery womb of my dolphin mother. I floated in the love of the Divine Mother while my body developed.

Minoan Majesty

What Minoans appeared to value most were unquantifiable things like joy, freedom, and dolphins. If there were any people who painted dolphins earlier, or more often, or more brilliantly, or exalted the animals more, we haven't yet found them. —Susan Casey (*Voices in the Ocean*, 2016)

I emerged from my mother's womb into a warm, aqua-blue sea. Sunlight streamed through the top of the water, lighting the white sand on the seafloor. Fish of all colors, coral, and interesting plants greeted my newborn eyes. I gazed upward, seeing the outline of majestic white limestone cliffs.

My mother and I swam toward the shore; I glided easily in her wake. The most beautiful human woman was standing on the rocks. She was wearing a white robe and offering flowers to the sea. We swam closer and the woman smiled at me. She waded more deeply into the water. A gold crown reflected light across her forehead.

I glided past her legs, weaving in and out as she lightly touched the top of my head and sprinkled me with flowers. The flowers tickled my back, and I laughed for the first time. I allowed her to touch my back and fins. She said, "Hello little one, my name is Johana," although her mouth didn't move. More humans met us, and my dolphin pod joined in the celebration. The joyous moment of my birth reunited our family of the land and sea. From the moment I arrived on Earth, I felt a deep and abiding connection with human beings.

It was a wonderful way to enter the world! Brilliant, in fact! I was born at a unique time in human history, when there was still reverence for the Divine Mother and all life. Your modern-day history books refer to this civilization as the ancient Minoans.

The Minoans lived in ancient Greece from about 3650 to 1400 B.C. They were a peaceful people with a goddess-centered culture. They worshiped the goddess Potnia, the mother of life. In modern times, you may call her Sophia or the Divine Mother, or by another name. The Minoans worshiped Potnia daily, and they honored dolphins as unique light beings on Earth and messengers of the mother (Casey, 2016). Living in alignment with the natural world, Minoans and dolphins communicated telepathically as great evolutionary partners. We shared mutual wisdom, cared for one another, and worshiped the divine together. You can still find evidence of our united cultures through their enduring art and structures. The Minoan temples still have beautiful frescoes of dolphins, and there are even underwater temples that remain on the ocean floor.

My human best friend's name was Aroc. He had brown hair and bright hazel eyes. We were about the same physical age and met daily at the shore. We played games and took grand adventures. When we were tired, we napped as I floated him on my back. We shared an unbreakable bond and loved each other as brothers. There are so many more stories about my lifetime in Minoa, but for now I only have time to share a glimpse with you.

The Oracles of Delphi

In the 5th century B.C., I was born in the gulf of Corinth in human form. I chose to live a life in service to the Oracles of Delphi mystery school. The Delphi lineage migrated to Greece from Egypt and India. This lineage held sacred divine feminine teachings and wisdom. The teachings of Delphi were created by the Divine Mother herself at a time when women carried matrilineal power through many generations.

My human mother was a temple oracle who lived in service to the Divine Mother and high dolphin councils. As a boy, I would watch as she swam into the gulf to meet the dolphins. After some time in the water, she ascended to a cave overlooking the sea, to meditate and receive their communications more fully. She was an incredible inspiration for me.

Our home was on the side of a vast mountain, a white adobe house built of limestone mud. We often traveled to the Delphic temple. The temple was built within a cave on a mountainside. It was quite a walk from our seaside village, but we went there at least three times a week. The temple grounds were beautifully designed through the use of sacred geometry, gardens, and a sacred spring. The temple grounds felt sacred, and the presence of Source pervaded my awareness when I entered the space. This was a sanctuary, a place of refuge and awakening for all beings. Wandering through the garden, I often witnessed water priestesses conducting ceremonies in the sacred springs.

The entry was marked by great white pillars and blooming bougainvillea vines. Above the entrance was the inscription "Know Thyself." When I was young, I did not understand what this saying meant, but as I grew from a boy to a man, I understood how these words remind us of the light of our true self, our identity as divine beings in physical form. This understanding is key for our divine liberation. Knowing our true selves is a key spiritual understanding. The wisdom of the Gnostics reflects this ancient divine feminine revelation, which will continue for eternity.

The cave was always dark when I entered, but then my eyes would adjust, revealing beautiful altars, pools of water, and light-language carvings. The main altar was a statue of the Divine Mother covered with beautiful flowers. At her feet, sapphire-blue water bowls were used to bless oneself or others. In the center of the temple was a deep pool of water fed by the sacred spring. The pool was round, with sapphire-blue stone tiles. There were large crystals growing within the cave, selenite and quartz, descending from the ceiling and walls. The crystals reflected the candle light beautifully.

Serving as a priest within the Delphic lineage, I trained in the wisdom of the divine feminine, learning many powerful practices. One of the most important was the art of interspecies communication. I lived many lifetimes in Delphi, until my last life, when I witnessed the dark forces take hold of my beloved sanctuary. This invasion marked the beginning of a shift on Earth that continues to this day.

Rise of the Darkness

In my final Delphic lifetime, I was born in the form of a human woman. Standing at the seashore, I observed ships on the horizon. Quickly ascending the staircase to tell the others, I felt fear pulsing through my body as I sensed impending doom. The priestesses remained calm, for they had knowledge from the oracles of what was to come. They immersed themselves in devotional prayers, speaking to the Divine Mother, asking for strength and blessings. Grabbing the shoulder of my dear friend,

I yelled, "Don't you understand? They are coming!" She simply smiled and said, "We will meet them with light and love. What else can we do?"

It felt like a nightmare as I watched the ships anchor, and heavily armed men began to approach our sacred land. Demonstrating no regard for the sanctity of life, they killed and destroyed everything in their path. Tears streamed down my face as I watched everything I loved shattered, including my own body.

The ancient myth "Hymn to Apollo" describes this very real invasion. The myth tells of how the god Apollo found the temple at Delphi at the foothills of Mount Parnassos. The cave was guarded by the dragoness Python, whom he slew with an arrow from his silver bow. The dragoness represents the divine feminine lineage that was sacrificed here. This myth holds the story of the decimation of the goddess cultures and the usurping of power by the destructive masculine. This myth tells us of the beginning of patriarchal control of the feminine.

Aside from this story, there is no record of this terrible event in modern times. As a story keeper, I was the guardian of this memory and knew I would share it when the time was right. What I witnessed is not different from what happened all over the world at this time. It was a terrible moment in history, or shall I say, "her story."

Luckily, physical death is not the end, and I vowed from the spirit realm that I would return to Gaia Earth again and again until the new era of peace began: a time when all beings would reclaim their divinity and freedom.

The Minotaur Myth

The story of my last human life is preserved in the myth of the Minotaur. Although the destructive masculine had seized control of the world, the heart of the divine feminine could not be extinguished. Slowly but surely, women began to reinstate practices of divine feminine consciousness.

My mother in this lifetime worked closely with the temple snakes, wrapping around her body as guardians. She worked closely with these Solstar beings, even sleeping with them. She was incredibly kind and raised me as an awakened human.

The great mission of my last human life was to help children. A great and terrible energy became embodied in the Minotaur, a monster created from the worst of mankind's darkness. He fed off anger, hatred, greed, and fear. He embodied great suffering and intense rage. Every year, he demanded that children be brought to him for sacrifice. I knew it was my life purpose to protect the children. Your present-day world is brutalizing and traumatizing children in a similar way. When the most vulnerable beings are hurt without regard, it is a sign that something has gone terribly wrong. You are here to do something about this and to make radical changes to ensure the safety and happiness of all children.

The families of Athens were terrified and lived under the shadow of the evil Minotaur. He lived on the island of Crete, and every year children were selected for sacrifice. A ship would sail them from Athens to Crete, in order to keep peace for the city. When I heard about this atrocity, I knew I must do something. I traveled to Athens, befriending a ship hand and securing a position onboard. I watched in horror as the children were selected and taken away from their parents. In this moment, I became absolutely committed to destroying the Minotaur and ending his reign of terror.

We set sail for Crete, and the cries of the children were unbearable. I went to the top deck of the ship to breathe, and a shape caught my eye. It was a dolphin swimming in the boat's current, jumping out of the water to get my attention. Then there were thousands of dolphins surrounding the ship. I knew this was a sign of my incredible support. Tears welling up in my eyes. I gazed at the water, knowing I would be victorious. The children noticed them too, their cries ceasing and smiles lighting up their faces.

Waking up the next morning, I was resolute in my mission. Rising in my dark and dusty room below deck, I dressed and armed myself. When I disembarked, I met eyes with one of the most beautiful women I've ever seen. She had long, dark brown hair and amber-colored eyes. Around her neck were a red scarf and a ruby pendant.

"I am Ariadne," she said.

I took her hand. "It is my pleasure to meet you. I am Theseus."

I fell in love with this beautiful woman instantly and knew I could trust her. I shared with her my secret mission, and upon hearing my intentions, she gave me a magical red thread to help me find my way out of the Minotaur's labyrinth.

The next morning, I helped escort the children to the labyrinth. I was told by the officials to leave them throughout the labyrinth for him to find and devour. As I walked them to the entrance, I whispered to each one that I would save them, and I asked them to be brave. Looks of hope washed across their faces.

I placed each child along the labyrinth and continued deep into the center to find the Minotaur. Along the way, I released my magical thread so I could find my way back out. The high, dark green walls of the labyrinth were made of hedgerows. Reaching the center, I prepared myself for battle.

"Who dares to trespass my inner sanctum?" boomed a severe and angry voice.

Waiting in the shadows, I steadied myself, summoning all of my courage.

"You will never leave this place now . . . no one ever has and no one ever will. I can smell you."

A dark figure emerged from a nearby cave. The Minotaur was a giant with a huge bull-shaped head. His red eyes glowed with hatred and anger. Horns sharp and black. Drawing my sword, I waited for him to come closer. My most important weapon was the element of surprise. Every muscle in my body tensed. I prayed to the divine goddess to help me defeat this terrible monster.

When he came close enough I sprang, knocking him off his feet. He screamed in anger and began kicking and flailing his arms. Realizing his vision was poor, I advanced toward his head. He knocked me away and my body crashed against a rock, my sword falling out of my hand. Standing above me, he raised a large rock, and I used my quick reflexes to locate my sword. I somersaulted, grabbed my sword, and leapt into the air. Everything stood still as I summoned my inner courage. My sword met its mark, smashing into the Minotaur's eye. He gasped, falling backward and taking his last breath before my eyes. I was victorious.

I followed Ariadne's thread to find my way out, collecting children along the way. One small boy took my face in his hands and said, "Thank you, dear sir; you have saved us all." The children ran toward me cheering, tears of happiness streaming down their faces. There were cries of relief, laughter, and triumphant giggles. I returned all the children safely to their families in Athens and became a revered leader. I used my political power to unify Athens, re-establishing the respect and honoring of all children.

The Vesica Pisces

I have lived during many unique times in history, witnessing the full spectrum of cultures. The beauty of the Minoans and wisdom of the Delphic order are some of my most favorite memories. Those times have planted seeds in the collective consciousness of what is possible for earthly life. If my stories resonate with you, there is a good possibility you were there too. Your soul does not forget. Your Higher Self retains the wisdom of all lifetimes. As you remember and integrate your lifetimes of service, your great purpose for this life is ignited. Let us step forward together as revolutionary leaders who are here to return the divine feminine to its rightful place on Earth.

The sacred geometric symbol of the Vesica Pisces holds sacred power. The symbol transmits divine feminine consciousness, making it a powerful healing tool. It transmits our inherent oneness, unity, connection, partnership, and relationship with the Divine Mother. It will help you remember your true and ancient self. Created long ago from matrilineal wisdom, this symbol represents many things: the goddess, the womb of all creation, the divine feminine, and oneness of heaven and Earth. I invite you to use this sacred geometric symbol as a healing tool in your daily life.

The Vesica Pisces is often referred to as the "womb fish," a term that refers to the mammal nature of both dolphins and humans. The Greek word *Delphi* ("dolphin") and *Depths* (meaning "womb") are very close. This is why I say this symbol signifies our unique connection. Humans and dolphins begin their life in the watery womb. Our bodies grow, protected within our mother, until we emerge on land or sea. We are family, and the Vesica Pisces reminds us of this. It will activate your memories and your connection to divine feminine consciousness. Place the symbol where you can see it regularly, or wear it on your clothing. I invite you to experience the transformative power this symbol holds. It symbolizes the power of creation itself.

The symbol is also inextricably linked to the Ocean Mother. The idea of divine feminine goddesses being connected to the sea permeates mythology all over the world. In China she is Quan Yin, and in India she is Kali, known as the fish-eyed one. In West Africa she is Yemana, goddess of the deep sea. The goddess Eurynome dances over the sea, creating order from chaos. Eurynome had a child, Themis, who was fish goddess and keeper of the Oracle of Delphi. Aphrodite is another goddess of the sea and moon. She was born on the island of Cyprus, and near her birthplace women established one of the most beautiful matrilineal societies called Paphos. A lesser-known version of Aphrodite's birth tells the story of how an egg fell from the sky into the water (probably referring to a meteorite). The egg was rescued by a dolphin, who brought it to shore.

Can you see all the beautiful feminine wisdom held within this symbol? Divine feminine consciousness is returning to its rightful place in this world. The Divine Mother offers her arms for comfort and gives you healing from her sacred heart. Her divine feminine energy will transform and heal all timelines.

Practices for Reclaiming Your Ancient Gifts

- Meditate, meditate, and meditate some more.
- Create sacred space for listening and just being in your life.
- Engage in present-moment practices like mindfulness.
- Read and study spiritual books that capture your attention. Notice what time periods in history you feel drawn to, because this magnetism is a clue, pointing you toward your wisdom. Watch for signs or synchronicities that guide you to study certain topics.
- Create altars with power objects and sacred items that help you remember your doorway to the divine.
- Learn about mythology, archetypes, and your inner masters. Discover the powerful ones within you. The healer, the wise one, the fool, the priest/priestess, the oracle, the scholar, the shaman, the spiritual teacher, the mystic, the artist— more than a few of them might be inside you.
- Invite your inner aspects to come out of the shadows. Let them know that in this life they are free to shine brightly and offer their gifts.
- Study ancient sacred geometry and see for yourself how symbols can be used to access unity consciousness and your Higher Self.
- Place the Vesica Pisces on your body through wearing clothing or using pens or paint. Put the symbol on your water bottle to charge the water with the power. Trust that you don't have to understand, simply receive.
- Connect with silver in your life through food, clothing, imagination, and environment. This color will assist you in restoring your ancient wisdom.
- Use the Scroll of Divine Wisdom daily to aid your self-remembrance and ancient gift activation.

Theseus Ancient Wisdom Remembrance Journey

The Prayer of Stella Maris

Divine Maha Ocean Mother:

Hold me in your warm embrace,
Float me in your cosmic ocean of grace.
Refresh me with your "I AM" presence,
Bless my waters with divine light and self-realization.
Weightless and suspended in light,
Wave after wave of divine love flows through my multidimensional form.
Vitality, health, and renewal restores me to my true self.
Receiving the light of the Divine Feminine.
Receiving the light of the Divine Masculine.
Healing balance within and without.
All parts of myself deeply loved.
No sound or movement, resting in your Oneness,
Great Mother of All of Life,
I remember who I am.
A starlight being, a beautiful creation of stardust and divine water light.
Living Divinity.
Surrounded by my divine family, I imagine the possible for all of life.
Returning to oneness,
I bless myself.
I love myself.
I know myself.
I am free.
I am my true self forevermore.

Stella Maris Speaks

Let us begin:

I place my hand on my heart and take three deep breaths. I am standing on the ocean floor, with the seawater rising seventy feet above me. The living water slowly begins to spin, creating a massive vortex around my body. Rays of light shine through the water, charging my body with electric energy. Stella Maris arrives, swimming in a circle around me. Boundless oceanic joy and rays of pink, aquamarine, and rainbow light emanate from their bodies. They flip, dive, laugh, and brush against me gently. The light touch tickles my skin, making me laugh bubbles. Whirling my body in a circle of light, the dolphins spin me in unison. They rotate my body to the right and then to the left. I allow myself to be moved, surrendering to their blessings. My heart feels at home here. I am pervaded by incredible happiness to have this opportunity to be with my sea family. The presence of the Great Divine Mother is here. She is all around me, and I float in her source field, returning to oneness. I close my eyes.

Mother Mary appears before me. She is wearing a dark blue cloak adorned with thousands of shining stars. She smiles and offers a warm embrace. I fall into her loving arms and she envelops me in brilliant white and pink light. She asks if I am ready to go on a visionary meditation with Theseus. I nod yes as she places her hands in mine. All becomes dark.

Before me stands a white limestone mountain, speckled with green trees and bushes. I remember this was once my home. My heart swells with happiness, knowing I have somehow found my way back. The white entry gate drips with scented jasmine flowers and is decorated with gold accents. This place is a sanctuary for my soul, a beloved location that exists beyond space and time. Standing in the doorway, I pause for a moment, taking in a deep breath and reflecting on my deep need to return and to remember the secrets here.

As I walk through the gate, the sound of water flows through my ears. A most beautiful garden comes into view, with stunning roses of every color and bright bougainvillea. The bougainvillea creates waterfalls of pink and orange flowers along the temple walls. The humming sound of bees surrounds me; they are singing a song of reunion. They buzz as one being, in perfect unison. Hummingbirds fly from flower to flower, drinking their nectar. There are rows of medicinal herbs—lavender, rosemary, and thyme. A breeze wafts toward me, filled with the scent of rose. Trees drip with olives, and the garden reveals an abundance of fruit and vegetables.

The sound of water beckons me closer, and I walk toward a circular fountain in the center. The fountain has a leaping dolphin sculpture, a round base made of beautiful blue tiles, and mosaics of humans and dolphins. Peering into the water, I feel a deep sense of peace. A sudden splash surprises me, and I watch in shock as a real dolphin rises from the depths of the water. It smiles—but how is this possible? Reaching into the water, I touch the top of its head. Quickly, the dolphin pushes its tail back and forth, rising up from the water. With a bright flash, the dolphin transforms into a man. He has dark hair, brown glowing eyes, and a sparkling smile. He wears a gold robe.

"I am Theseus," he says. "It is a pleasure to meet you."

I am stunned, and I try to understand what I have just witnessed. He continues to speak. "I am your guide. I will help you remember who you are and where you came from." A sense of excitement flows through me, and my stomach churns with butterflies.

"Do you wish to remember?"

"Yes," I state loudly. "I have been waiting for this moment for all my life."

"Welcome to your temple!" Theseus exclaims. We walk toward a beautiful white building built into the limestone mountains. There are large white columns and carved steps at its entrance.

"Do you know your sanctuary has always been close?" Theseus smiles. "My mission is to help you remember your connection so you can access the wisdom of your many lifetimes. I am a story keeper, and I know your lineage, past, and gifts that transcend time. You are now able to bring your ancient knowledge and wisdom through to your present life. Isn't it great? Nothing has been lost! All of your wisdom has been stored in the light of your heart.

"Your knowledge is critical at this moment on Earth, for it holds the keys to our collective evolution and freedom. You are an unlimited being, existing simultaneously as your ancient, current, and future self. You are a true multidimensional being. You seem to be traveling in a linear timeline, and yet you have already arrived at your destination. At the end of the never-ending road there is only love. In your current human lifetime, it is important for you to remember your past."

We continue walking along the pathway, as I try to absorb what I am hearing.

"We have lived many lifetimes where the human and dolphin connection was strong and the Great Divine Mother was known and revered."

We reach the steps of the temple. Beautiful women in pure white dresses line the steps. They smile at me, bowing their heads in reverence. I feel like a queen or king who is honored by my friends. We climb the marble steps and reach the inside of the temple. It is elliptical, with an elevated roof where the sun shines through prismatic glass. The floors are made of stunning tile mosaics that show stories of dolphins and humans through time.

A round pool sits in the center of the temple, fed by the fresh water of a sacred spring. The deep azure-blue pool in the center is gorgeous and beckons me closer. I notice how the water emerges from the mountain cool and clear, flowing through carved channels in the floor and into the pool. After swirling in the pool, it continues to flow through four direction channels and out to the garden.

The scent of frankincense, herbs, roses, and incense wafts through the air as I take in the beauty of the temple. A woman slowly approaches to my right. She has an albino snake wrapped around each of her arms. The snakes raise their heads to greet me, their tongues flicking happily. She motions me toward the circular pool in the center. Standing in the pool are four women in white robes. I recognize them from the temple stairs. They invite me to enter, and I slowly walk down the steps, noticing how I am wearing a white robe too. The robe floats in the water, billowing around me as I take each step. The pool is deep. I am invited to float on my back, held by the strength of their arms. Sunlight streams in from the top of the temple. My ears rest below the water; it is peaceful and quiet. The water is warm and inviting, as the women begin to sing. Beautiful voices are flowing over me in time with the water's waves.

"We, the Oracles of Delphi, invoke the presence of the Divine Mother to join us now for this healing ceremony. We invite Stella Maris and all of the past wisdom keepers of Delphi." I close my eyes, seeing the vision of a circle of light beings gathering around me. The women begin to sing: "May you remember who you are, may you know your true self. May you heal and realign, so you can easily bring your ancient wisdom forward into this life. May you be blessed, may you walk the Beauty Way. May you live as your highest self, participating in your highest divine service."

They begin to speak in Ancient Greek, a language I do not understand. "Να θυμάσαι ποιος είσαι." Remember who you are. Remember who you are. Remember who you are. They place their hands on each of my chakras, aligning my energy. First, they place their hands on my heart chakra, then on the top of my head, followed by my throat, third eye, solar plexus, sacral, and root chakras. They hold my hands and feet for several minutes.

Ascended master Quan Yin appears by my feet, wearing a flowing white and gold robe. Her black hair is tied back, and she smiles at me with sparkling dark brown eyes. She holds my feet, sending a pulse of electric energy through my body. The white gold light flows from her hands into my form. The water is alive; I can feel its presence and equanimity. It sways me gently from side to side. Quan Yin releases my feet. In her delicate hand, she holds a crystal bottle. Uncorking the lid, she releases a rainbow mist that flows in all directions.

A white mist descends above my head, filling me with the white ray of pure light. A royal purple mist flows over my body, and I inhale the moist royal medicine of honor and nobility. A red mist descends through me, bringing a sense of safety, energy, and empowerment. An orange mist brings me joy, the energy of play and bright happiness. A yellow mist blesses me with a feeling of courage and strength. A green mist envelops me with the feeling of deep love and self-compassion. A lilac purple mist tickles my throat, and I laugh out loud. A blue mist brings clarity and communication, opening my throat chakra and clearing my expressive channels. A deep indigo mist gathers around my third eye, clearing my psychic ability and my inner vision channels. It flows through my form, aligning me and restoring perfect balance. At last, pink and aquamarine mists flow over me, bringing feelings of delight and excitement. All the colors join together, creating a bright, pure white light. I receive the healing on all levels of my being.

The women begin their song once again. "May you be healed. May you remember. May you awaken, may you speak truth. May you remember who you are, may you know yourself as the Divine One. May you have deep self-compassion and self-love. May you know your divinity and royalty. May you return to oneness. May you live your divinity. May you walk the Beauty Way."

The prayers activate a new awareness within me, and I feel myself integrating more of my Higher Self. The voices slowly fade, and when I open my eyes, the women and snakes are gone. I am held by an invisible force, which floats me in the water. My Divine Mother. Deeply relaxed, I close my eyes, falling into a deep sleep. Weightless and formless, I dissolve into the oneness of the light.

After some time, I become aware of my body again. A rush of moving water awakens me. I realize I have transformed into a dolphin. I swim in circles, feeling a balance and fluidity unlike anything I have experienced in human form. Two dolphins join me, and we swim back and forth in the pool. They sing to me with their high voices. I feel so happy! Their sonar language of light bubbles up, landing on my dolphin body. I join the song with my own dolphin voice, feeling in complete balance, like I have always known how to exist in this way.

The dolphins place their bodies next to mine and guide me to the stairs. It is time to leave. Thanking them, I place my forehead against theirs, and as I take my first step, my body changes effortlessly back into my human form. Shining brightly and dripping with sacred water, I leave the pool. Theseus is standing close, smiling.

"Don't worry, you can come back whenever you like."

He places a scroll in my hand and transforms into a dolphin, diving into the temple pool and disappearing from sight.

I cross the threshold of the temple and blink as the sunlight shines in my eyes. The temple fades and Mother Mary takes my hand, embracing me once more. "Now it is time to return," she says kindly. As we part, Mother Mary kisses a white rose and places it behind my ear. I slowly unroll the scroll and read aloud:

The Scroll of Ancient Wisdom

Standing in the power and peace of my divinity, I proclaim:

My true nature is alive and well

I recognize myself as a being of light

I am a divine master in human form

My energetic balance is restored

I honor the gifts of my ancient wisdom

Nothing was ever lost

I return all of my gifts for use in my current experience

I am always able to connect to home

I activate my highest divine purpose for the good of all beings

I am fully supported by my family and the Divine Mother herself

I reclaim all parts of my soul that have been fractured
or seemingly lost because of past experiences or suffering

I bring myself back to myself in all dimensions of space and time,
and all levels of being

I am healed

I now clear all of my intuitive channels

Where my soul is stuck or lost, it breaks free, returning fully to me

I am a divine oceanic being of love

I remember who I am

I am indestructible light and hold within me the innocence of pure being

I restore my power

I activate my voice

I am whole

Breathing in the rainbow mist of freedom,
I am fully here now, living as my true self forevermore

And so it is

Chapter 16
Mahadra
Messenger of Divine Healing

Mahadra Speaks:

My name is Mahadra, which means "one flowing source." I am a healer and water priestess, and my name signifies my connection to the holy waters of the Divine Mother. Deeply connected to the living being of water, I honor this source of all life. I work with water's incredible healing properties daily. I bless you with the aquamarine ray of divine healing and offer you teachings of how to connect with the consciousness of water. Your relationship with water is a very important part of how you can heal the Earth. I have one daughter, Kaleosi, who you have already met. It is one of my greatest delights to guide my daughter.

Quan Yin is my dear friend. She lived on the island of Pu Tuo, which is where we first met. In modern times, she is often depicted riding on the back of a dolphin and holding a water vessel in her hand, symbolizing her healing work with water and divine feminine consciousness. It is said that she pours the waters of compassion and self-love from a seemingly empty chalice. She will assist me with my messages and will participate in our visionary meditation.

My Message for You

Your body is made of water, and as such, is alive and responsive to water healing. Every time you drink, bathe, swim, or rest near bodies of water, you are re-uniting with Source energy. Bless yourself with the rivers, lakes, oceans, and rain. Create healing intentions for the water. In ancient times, wise women went to the water daily to connect with the Divine Mother and receive her messages. Water is a sacred medium that can be used for blessings, radical healing, and transformation. As a practitioner of the water arts, I am delighted to share my knowledge with you. You can receive healing through all of water's forms, including the form of your own body. You are intimately connected to water as the most important element for your continued life.

Each beat of your heart creates waves through your body. Seawater blood flows through your veins, renewing and refreshing your life force. Place your hands on your heart. Feel the waves flowing from your heart to the tips of your fingers and toes. You are a living ocean! You are water that has left its banks and can walk in the holy chalice of your human form. How amazing!

The element of water can heal all levels of your being—physical, emotional, mental, and heart/soul. Physically, you can work with the water through intention and immersion. Emotionally, water can help you feel your emotions within the chalice of your body—a profound act of self-love. Water can help you shift your thought patterns, cultural conditioning, and beliefs, replacing them with healthier and more true ones as you pray and set intentions over the water you drink. You are a water being, so it can also help to heal your soul and the deepest recesses of your heart. As you develop a closer relationship to water, you will understand that it is a dear friend and ally for all life. I will teach you how to work with water as a healing medium.

Hopefully this connection will help you to take action to protect and bless the waters of Gaia Earth. Years of pollution have negatively impacted the Earth's water, but it is not too late.

The Genius of Dr. Masaru Emoto

Dr. Masaru Emoto was a pioneer in the field of vibrational water healing. Through his work, Dr. Emoto demonstrated how water responds to intentions and thoughts. His close-up photography of water crystals showed how words, thoughts, and external pollutants have a profound effect on the vibration and structure of water (www.Hado.com, 2016).

Dr. Emoto did a series of experiments throughout the 1990s. He took microscope pictures of the structure of water after it was exposed to both positive and negative intentions. The results were quite remarkable. The water given positive intent organized itself into beautiful crystalline structures, while the water that was polluted or given negative intentions became very disorganized. Through his photography, Dr. Emoto showed how words and thoughts clearly impact the crystalline structure of water, proving water is a conscious and responsive element. Near the end of his life, Dr. Emoto created "Angel Water," which he infused with love and gratitude. He gave this water to children after the nuclear accident in Japan to help neutralize radiation. Many of the children experienced healing (www.Hado.com, 2016).

The Creator called upon me to be a voice for the water. Water is sacred and is our first medicine. I teach people to thank the water every day of your life. The river, the lake near your house, the glass of water you are holding in your hand. Tell the water, "Bless me. I love you." —Grandmother Agnes Baker Pilgrim

Water Is Your Physical Form

Water is an essential part of your physical form. Your body is 60 to 70 percent water. Babies and children have an even higher percentage of water, an astounding 65 to 78 percent! Your heart and brain are made of 73 percent water, and your lungs are 83 percent water. As a baby, you develop in a watery womb environment. Your body floats because it has the same density as water, with your mineral composition the same as the ocean. (*Blue Mind,* Wallace J. Nichols). Water is the primary building block of your cells and regulates your internal body temperature, digests your food, and lubricates your joints. Water insulates your brain, spinal cord, and organs. Water is used to flush waste and toxins from the body. The human body has intrinsic healing abilities and uses water to repair and rebuild its form.

Water Healing Practices for Your Greatest Well-Being

Your physical body needs clean water for optimal vitality. Most drinking water has been tainted with environmental pollutants, medications, and chemicals. I advise you to invest in a water filtration system or to get your water from a pure source. You can even purchase water filters for bathing. Drink at least 10 glasses of water a day to allow your body to flush out toxins. Infuse your water with intentions for healing. For example, you can hold your hand over the water glass and say "joy" or "vitality," and the energy of your intention will infuse the water. Your food is also composed of water, so blessing your food and eating with intention also has a profound healing impact on your body. I recommend eating the purest food you can find. Eat organic, non-GMO foods; genetic modification can change the cellular structure in the food, making it toxic to your cells. Bless and pray over your food and it will respond by nourishing your body.

You can draw toxins out of your body through bathing. You can use baking soda and sea salt, apple cider vinegar, and aromatherapy oils in your bath. Be sure to state your intention before entering the bath by holding your hands over the water's surface. You can use one word or several sentences to bless and energize the water. Soaking in water can rebalance your body system and invigorate your crystalline structure. Immersion in water has been used for healing since ancient times. You can add fresh flowers or plants such as rose petals, crystals or gemstones, and essential oils. You can also speak your prayers or intentions to the water in your shower. Speak to your friend as it flows before you.

Immersing yourself in an ocean, lake, or river is one of the most health promoting activities you can participate in. Dive in! This will bring amazing changes to your vitality and health. Visit a larger body of water like the ocean or a lake at least once a month. Choose places where the water flows freely and is pure and charged with negative ions, important particles that will recharge your life force. Many diseases start at the cellular level in the crystalline water structure of your form. Water is the electrical conductor within the body. In my experience, you develop disease when your inner water is toxified by environmental toxins, emotional states, or thoughts. By consciously working with water, you can minimize these potential negative impacts and create healing.

Your Mental Body and Water

Your mental body is made up of a stream of thoughts—pun intended! You can elevate your health by becoming conscious and aware of your thoughts and the impact they are having. Your thoughts have an immediate impact on your reality and the water within your body. When you become conscious of this, you will choose new ways of thinking. Do you speak negatively or positively to yourself? Are you critical of yourself and your body? What is your worldview, and what beliefs do you hold? Your thoughts are constantly changing the cellular structure of your form, because water within you is responsive and conscious. I invite you to become aware of the thoughts and beliefs that are causing you disturbance and disharmony.

In Dr. Emoto's work, the thought "you disgust me" was reflected in a disorganized and chaotic crystalline structure in the water, while the thought "I love you" created a beautiful crystalline snowflake. What happens when you participate in negative self-talk? The water in your body is literally being polluted.

You can change your thoughts in many ways. You can use affirmations, you can become aware of thoughts and shift them. You can use positive thoughts to direct health to your body. For example, "I deeply love and accept myself; all of my cells are healing and recharging at this moment; my body is filled with healing."

Closely guard your mind, making conscious choices about the information you will allow into your mind. World news, tragedy, negative television, and violent movies can create toxicity in your mind by traumatizing you, entrapping you in others' belief structures, and polluting your inner waters. Humanity's collective fear can wreak havoc on the water bodies of Earth, creating hurricanes and other disharmonies of weather. In your information age, please be mindful of what you are absorbing mentally and the amount of time you spend on screens and devices. Some say the electromagnetic frequencies of your cell phones and computers can create ill health and diminish your body's healing ability.

Your Emotional Body

The Guest House

This being human is a guest house.
Every morning a new arrival.
A joy, a depression, a meanness,
some momentary awareness comes
as an unexpected visitor.
Welcome and entertain them all!
Even if they're a crowd of sorrows,
who violently sweep your house
empty of its furniture,
still treat each guest honorably.
He may be clearing you out
for some new delight.
The dark thought, the shame, the malice,
meet them at the door laughing,
and invite them in.
Be grateful for whoever comes,
because each has been sent
as a guide from beyond.
—Rumi

Emotions have long been associated with water. Your body is a living chalice for your feelings. Being human means experiencing a range of human emotions. Bless this part of earthly life. When you reject or suppress a "negative" feeling it stays within your body, waiting for its chance to be expressed. If you allow yourself to feel all of your feelings and honor them with love and compassion, they will move through like a passing storm. But if you fight or resist the feelings, they may sneak up and crush you! Can you can honor and love each feeling as it arises within you? What feeling is arising to be loved next? Allow all of your feelings: the sorrow, the joy, the anger, the fear, the happiness, and everything in between. Feelings carry wisdom and messages teaching you how to deeply love all aspects of yourself. Your ability to create space for your feelings allows them to alchemize and transform. Experiencing all of your feelings is one of the highest divine feminine practices. Ask for help from your Higher Self when you are lost in emotional waters. Your willingness to feel blesses your inner waters beyond measure, creating multidimensional health.

Your inner children offer important insights into your emotional body. They often carry unhealed feelings from childhood. When you were young, you may have been told feelings were bad. You may have subconsciously internalized and reenacted this same intolerance and rejection of feelings. Awareness can heal. You may realize that many of your feelings stem from the little ones within who simply need love, acceptance, and comfort.

Your Heart Connection to Water and the Power of Prayer

Your electromagnetic heart sings to the vibration of water because you arose from the one cosmic Ocean Mother. Your soul is deeply connected to water, so I invite you to honor this relationship. Your conscious relationship with water allows you to commune with your own essence, creating health, balance, and happiness. Your spiritual nature has the same qualities of water as it flows with grace. Drink deeply of your divinity, knowing your own being.

I invite you to make water prayers and intentions part your daily life. Prayer is one of the highest divine feminine healing medicines. There is no right way to pray—choose your own way. Imagine all of your cells infused with health and light. Pray for your thoughts, emotions, inner child, and your divine soul. Pray for others, including your loved ones, community, and Gaia Earth herself. Take the time to bless yourself and the living being of water.

Water Advocacy

You are a water being, living on a water planet. In the last thousand years, Gaia Earth's water has become polluted and sick. I invite you to become an advocate for water. Water is the source of all life. Stand up for this most precious elemental being. Protect your beautiful, holy water. Join others to stop contamination and pollution. Participate in movements or projects that provide clean water. Stand up against corporations who try to control the world's fresh water and pollute the Earth's rivers, lakes, and oceans. Practice environmentalism within your own home and teach others how you work with water. Participate in world water-blessing ceremonies. Choose any form of advocacy that works for you, for as you heal the water, you also heal yourself and all beings.

Creating Water Elixirs for Healing

I invite you to create water elixirs for healing, as a daily way to connect with the living being of water and its extraordinary healing power.

General guidelines for creating water elixirs:
- Use water from a natural spring source or water that has been filtered. The water can be fresh or salt, depending on how you will be working with it.
- Water elixirs are best made in glass containers, rather than plastic or synthetic materials.
- Ask the water to assist you; water is always happy to help.
- Decide what intention or prayer you wish to impart into the water. You can hold your hand over the water and send energy through your hand. You can speak prayers out loud or say them silently within.

Moon Water and Sun Water

Moon water is a powerful divine feminine water elixir. The moon is closely connected with all waters on Earth, even commanding the tides of the sea. Each phase of the moon offers different healing qualities for infusing water. Fill your bottles with pure water and place them in the moonlight. Be sure to place them outside after the sun has set. Leave your water in the moonlight for a minimum of two to three hours or for the entire night. Collect the water and store it in a cool, dark place before the sun rises. Sunlight will alter the moon essence that has been imbued into the water.

Moon water holds divine feminine transmissions and is particularly useful for self-love, healing of emotions, balance within the body, self-care, restoration of the cells, and self-compassion. Moon water can also bring you joy and happiness, and return your sense of humor.

Sun Water

Sun water is a highly charged divine masculine elixir of life. You can place your clear glass or colored bottles on a windowsill or outside, allowing the water to absorb the sun rays. Sun water can be helpful with energy, strength, courage, activation of goals, leadership, and wisdom. Sun water can give you energy and dynamic joy. I recommend placing your water out in the morning, so it can catch the rising sun rays. Place your bottle in the sunlight for at least two to three hours or for the entire day. The sun has long provided incredible healing benefits, and when the light is infused into water, the sky is the limit!

Star Water

Ancient matrilineal cultures created star water. Place your water outside, when the moon is waning or new. Choose constellations based on your intuition or astrological knowledge. Look at the stars, asking for blessings and stating your intention for your water. Different constellations and star systems hold different healing energies. For example, in India they believe awakened masters reside in Ursa Major and this star water can bless spiritual development and bring wisdom. You can make star water in November when the Pleiades are shining bright and ask for blessing and healing from Stella Maris. Be creative in your star connections!

Color Water

You can create healing elixirs with color. Use colored glass water bottles to infuse water. Each color holds a healing ray and vibrational healing. Choose colors based on your intuition or use the chakra color system. Chakras are energy centers that are located on different parts of your body. These energy centers oscillate, fanning life force energy through your body. Your root chakra is located at the base of your spine and is the color red. Orange is the color of the sacral chakra, yellow is the color of the solar plexus chakra, green is the color of the heart chakra, light blue/turquoise is the color of the throat chakra, indigo is the color of the third eye chakra, purple is the color of the crown chakra, and white light emanates above the head as your Higher Self chakra. If you are having a particular health challenge, you can infuse the water with a color that helps with the corresponding area of the body.

You can use prayer or intention with color water. For example, if you are having digestive problems, I recommend using an orange bottle and praying for ease and comfort. Then drink! Another fun type of water is rainbow water, which is created by mixing all the different colors together from the bottles. Use your creativity and intuition—the possibilities for healing water are endless!

Stella Maris Blessing Labels

You can use symbols and words to bless your food, drink, and water. Many powerful sacred geometric symbols have been used as powerful healing tools. This includes light language symbols, which are useful to infuse the energy of your water and environment. Create interesting and unique combinations for your healing. Here we suggest eight symbols that are special to our offerings for your use: infinity, Vesica Pisces, spiral, Merkaba, sacred star, heart, dolphin circle, and trinity.

Sound Water

Music and sound have a profound effect on the structure of water. When you play music, water resonates and responds to its sound. You can use different kinds of music for specific intentions. You can also play instruments next to the water with intention, such as crystal bowls, harps, guitars, pianos, or other instruments of beauty. Study how different musical notes correspond to chakras in the body. For example, the note F resonates with the heart chakra. Sound infuses the water with healing vibrations. Drink and enjoy!

Flower and Plant Water

The healing practice of using plants and flowers to infuse water is an incredible healing tool that has been lost in modern-day society. In this century, Dr. Edward Bach rediscovered how to create water essences with plants, trees, and flowers. Following his inner guidance, Dr. Bach left his successful medical practice and moved to the country, where he immersed himself in the creation of remedies. He believed physical sickness resulted from a disharmony between mind and body and that the essence of plants, trees, and flowers could restore this balance. Bach developed many flower remedies that continue to heal many people. Bach describes his process of creating elixirs:

> *A thin glass bowl is taken and almost filled with the purest water obtainable, if possible from a spring nearby. The blooms of the plant are picked and immediately floated on the surface of the water, so as to cover it, and then left in the bright sunshine for three or four hours, or less time if the blooms begin to show signs of fading. The blossoms are then carefully*

lifted out and the water poured into bottles so as to half fill them. The bottles are then filled up with brandy to preserve the remedy. These bottles are stock, and are not used direct for giving doses.

A note of caution: Make sure every plant, flower, or tree you are using for your elixir is edible. If you do not want to use alcohol to preserve, just remember to drink the water within a few days or store at a cool temperature. You can also place water at the base of a tree and allow the energetic signature of the tree to infuse the water without using actual leaves or bark. You do not necessarily have to pick or take parts of the plant. You can also infuse the water by placing it next to flowers or plants and setting an intention to infuse the water with its essence.

Gem water

Crystals and stones can be used to infuse water. First, study the properties of the gem or crystal to make sure it's not toxic. Place the crystal or stone in or near the water with intention. Some crystals work well with moonlight and others work well with sunlight. Follow your intuition! Leave the crystal or stone in the water for two to twelve hours. Store the water in a cool place. Rivers naturally infuse stones and crystals. You can re-charge or clear your crystals in larger bodies of water.

Mahadra Divine Water Healing Journey

The Prayer of Stella Maris

Divine Maha Ocean Mother:

Hold me in your warm embrace,
Float me in your cosmic ocean of grace.
Refresh me with your "I AM" presence,
Bless my waters with divine light and self-realization.
Weightless and suspended in light,
Wave after wave of divine love flows through my multidimensional form.
Vitality, health, and renewal restores me to my true self.

16: Mahadra—Messenger of Divine Healing

Receiving the light of the Divine Feminine.
Receiving the light of the Divine Masculine.
Healing balance within and without.
All parts of myself deeply loved.
No sound or movement, resting in your Oneness,
Great Mother of All of Life,
I remember who I am.
A starlight being, a beautiful creation of stardust and divine water light.
Living Divinity.
Surrounded by my divine family, I imagine the possible for all of life.
Returning to oneness,
I bless myself.
I love myself.
I know myself.
I am free.
I am my true self forevermore.

Let us begin:

I place my hand on my heart and take three deep breaths. I am standing on the ocean floor as Stella Maris circles above me. They swim clockwise, creating a whirlpool of water, spinning my body in a vortex of light. Glancing at my chest, I discover a blue crystal that helps me to breathe easily underwater. Mahadra swims up, floating beside me. She motions for me to look up at Quan Yin, who is floating just above the water. She wears an aqua-blue robe, with her hair drawn up, a few strands blowing across her face. Mahadra invites me for a healing ceremony. I transform into my dolphin body, following her through the ocean water. Quan Yin follows us above. Beautiful white stone cliffs rise like a mystical cathedral against the bright blue sky. Just as we reach the shoreline we dive deep, entering a circular tunnel. Darkness surrounds us, and I feel calm, full of trust. A glowing light appears, signaling for us to rise to the surface. We emerge in a sapphire-blue, circular pool. The blue color is otherworldly, and on all sides limestone cliffs rise out of the water in a perfect circle.

Quan Yin softly lands on a cliff nearby. She raises her arms to the effervescent blue sky to begin the ceremony. Mahadra swims in circles around me as I lie on my back, my body held by the buoyancy of the saltwater. I am now in my human form. Mahadra speaks: "Welcome to the ceremony of divine water healing. We have created this activation to heal you. Let us begin: . . ." As my body spins slowly on the top of the water, I watch Quan Yin burn incense and myrrh. She sprinkles water from her crystal-blue chalice onto a basket of white flower petals. Holding the basket next to her heart, she blesses the petals and begins to toss handfuls into the water. The flower petals float slowly, suspended by an unknown force. They dance and swirl in the wind.

Quan Yin begins to sing "Om Mane Padme Hum, Om Mane Padme, Hum" as the flowers gently land on my body, covering me from head to toe. They create a beautiful image of the water's surface. The smell of rose, tuberose, peony, and jasmine fill my awareness. The petals glow with color, as if they are each lit by an inner flame.

"I heal your sight and vision with the blue ray and white flowers." I close my eyes and see brilliant hues of blue: sapphire, blue-green, royal blue, aqua, sea green, baby blue, and turquoise. The colors wash over me in waves, covering my body with light. White flower petals dance around me, brushing my body with their soft petals. The blue water and flower beings sparkle together, shining like a thousand diamonds.

"I heal your hearing with the crystalline sounds of light." The sound of crystal singing bowls is all around me as I rest in the oneness consciousness amplified by sound. Sounds of singing angels, ocean waves, waterfalls, and flowing creeks pass through my ears. The joyful sound of singing birds, playing dolphins, and whale songs grace my awareness. Then it is quiet, the sound of pure unity.

"I heal your sense of touch." A thousand healing hands are holding and cradling me in loving light. The hands facilitate advanced energy healing through their movement. Brilliant sparks flow out of the hands, and I see the presence of angels. My experience of separation dissolves, and I can't remember where I begin or end. I return to my body when a soft feather tickles my forehead.

"I heal your sense of taste." My mouth delights in the taste of the most delicious fruits: ripe orange, mango, sweet strawberry, and juicy pink guava. My favorite gourmet meal appears before me, and I taste the luscious food as if for the first time, eating ravenously and receiving the highest nourishment.

"I heal your sense of smell." My favorite flower scents waft through the air: tuberose, plumeria, gardenia, hyacinth, rose, and lilac. The smells of clean air, water, fresh rain, burning candles, baking bread, and simmering soup enthrall my senses.

"I heal your intuitive channels and extrasensory perception." With my third eye, I envision beautiful waterfalls of rainbow light. I am flying over the ocean and merging into a golden sunset. The gold has its own sound and vibration and whispers to me the secrets of life. My dream world appears before me, lucid and clear, filled with symbolism of my Higher Self. I can easily understand my dream messages.

"I heal your self-esteem." Overwhelming love and light enter my body, and I feel immense self-love. I fall in love with myself over and over, seeing the light of my pure heart.

"I heal your thoughts and belief systems." My old thoughts and beliefs fly out, exiting my head and appearing as hundreds of written pages. I read them all simultaneously, surprised by the subconscious contents of my mind. I recognize how thoughts have hindered me and kept me in suffering. Embracing long-awaited freedom, I witness the pages of my old thoughts dissolve in the Source water.

"I seal this healing through all space and time," says Quan Yin. Opening my eyes, I witness Quan Yin and Mahadra casting water droplets from the vase into the air. "Om, Om, Om," Quan Yin chants above me. A golden-white-light version of myself floats down from the higher realms. She merges her energy with mine. I feel renewed. It is my Higher Self. The most sacred part of me has been returned and is integrated more fully. I slowly open my eyes. Night has fallen; the sky is dark blue with twinkling stars. Quan Yin stands on my right and Mahadra to my left. They smile, shining with pride. Mahadra swims close and wraps her fins around my body. I thank her and shower her with flowers from the pool. I express my gratitude and appreciation to Quan Yin, bowing to honor her incredible gifts to me. We begin our journey home, floating effortlessly above the smooth ocean water. I notice a scroll in my hand. I unroll it and read aloud:

The Scroll of Divine Water Healing

Standing in the power and peace of my divinity, I proclaim:

Water is a powerful element of divine feminine healing

I invoke the power and presence of the living water to heal me now

When I heal my waters, I heal all waters on Earth

Water is the elemental source of all of life

When I speak to the water, it receives my prayers
and the water answers by changing its very structure into beautiful crystals

I am a crystal

I am water

Placing my hand on my heart, I speak to the water within myself:
I love you, I bless you

——

I am a pure and holy human being

I am an angel on Earth

I am the blessing

I now choose unlimited beauty, perfect alignment, joy and laughter,
incredible abundance, divine purpose, and love

I am a divine being of water light

Every cell of my body is infused with healing

I heal all of my senses now

I accept the healing of my vision and sight

I accept the healing of my sense of smell

I accept the healing of my thoughts and beliefs

I accept the healing of my touch

I accept the healing of my hearing

I accept the healing of my taste

I accept the healing of my intuition

I accept the healing of my self-concept

I accept these healings with gratitude and grace

I activate my newly restored senses and use them with ease

I accept this healing into all of my energetic bodies

I honor myself

I reclaim myself

I remember myself

I love myself

I understand that water is an unparalleled medium
for personal and planetary healing

May the water of all beings and the waters of Gaia Earth
be healed, restored, and blessed

Chapter 17
Grandmother Izoma and Grandfather Skylan
Messengers of Divine Balance and Alignment

Elders Izoma and Skylan Speak:

We are Grandmother Izoma and Grandfather Skylan, elders of Stella Maris who are here to help you with divine alignment. We bless you, healing from the indigo blue ray and our light language. Let us begin by explaining why alignment is so important.

Our Message for You

As a human being, you have two brain hemispheres: the left and right. Your corpus callosum is the connection between these two hemispheres, and functions like a bridge for information. Your right brain correlates with your feminine energy, the place you access emotions and the power of creativity. Your left brain is the seat of masculine energy, where you access logic, language, and reasoning. We are here to help you create a harmonious inner balance. These two seemingly opposite energies can dance in balance like the yin-yang symbol so beautifully shows. When they are in balance, your human awareness can operate optimally as it rests in the consciousness of your Higher Self.

In your current world, the human left brain/masculine has been more valued than the right brain/feminine. The left brain is regarded as the center of power through its logical reasoning, speech, language, memory, and sequence. The feminine right brain is not as valued, even though it is the seat of creativity, visual imagery, emotional intelligence, and imagination. The left brain can be described as experiencing the world in black and white and from the perspective of "I," while the right brain experiences infinite colors and a "we" perspective.

As dolphins, we exist in complete brain equanimity and balance. We access our right and left brain capacity at will. We use our abilities in service to our hearts. We have incredibly advanced brain capacity, because our brains have literally been rewired by unity consciousness. Your scientists are just discovering how evolved our brains really are. We are models of what is possible for you.

We do not sleep; when we need to rest we simply choose to move our awareness to one side of our brain. This allows us to simultaneously rest and maintain consciousness. We experience the seamless balance of our masculine and feminine energies. We even breathe consciously. Our physical form reflects this seamless brain alignment. That is why it is difficult to tell the difference between female and male dolphins by simply observing our physical appearance.

We witness that many modern humans are taught to be overly dominant in their left brain and masculine attributes. When you are trapped in left brain dominance you can become cut off from your heart and emotions, which creates the experience of isolation. Your loneliness disconnects you from your inherent joy and happiness.

The use of computers and electronic devices keeps you locked in your left brain function. The left brain is important, but not meant to be the primary place from which you operate. The left brain is most useful if offered in service to your heart and Higher Self. It is most helpful when in balance with the right brain. Without the balancing force of your right brain and heart, the unhealthy masculine left brain can create much suffering. The left brain can keep you imprisoned in repetitive thoughts, where you live as a glorified robot, completing your tasks and making logical and predictable choices within a narrow range of possibility. Your current patriarchal system of power relies on keeping you trapped in left-brain belief systems. It fosters the perception that you are all alone, an individual, and that you must compete with others. Your consumer culture is entirely based on this belief structure and creates power through fear and valuing control over others. When you dominantly operate from your left brain, the energy within your body does not flow freely, and your energy circuits can become blocked. Balance and alignment between your energy and brain function allows the energy to descend and circulate as it was designed to within your body. This brings health, clarity, and well-being.

You are undergoing a radical change on Earth as the divine feminine returns. The current belief systems will be shattered, because they do not benefit the whole. The divine feminine knows the truth: Every being and form is the one Source. We are all in this together. There is no true separation; we are a family of light. We are interdependent, not separate. We are connected.

By prioritizing the development of your right-brain function and inner divine feminine aspects, you can create balance that allows your Higher Self to integrate more fully. You will be able to access more of your capabilities and experience wholeness. Your balance will bring peace and equanimity to the world. There are many ways to develop your right brain and inner feminine aspects, so we invite you to follow the path that brings you the most joy.

Creative expression is a direct pathway to accessing your right brain. All forms of expression strengthen your right-brain ability, including art, music, writing, cooking, photography, crafting, and dance. Your right-brain awareness is fully immersed in the now. Practice using your senses to bring yourself into the present moment through sight, smell, hearing, touch, taste, and intuition. We invite you to cultivate your right-brain-ability awareness and your feminine energy, whether you are male or female. Your brain alignment can activate your creativity, intuition, joy, and imagination. Right-brain activation will also open your channel for interspecies communication, telepathy, and extrasensory perceptions. Your divine feminine consciousness invites you to experience life in alignment.

You can also engage in spiritual practices that develop mindfulness, activate your inner feminine, and balance your brain. This includes meditation, guided visualization, chi gong, yoga, sound healing, spiritual practices, and martial arts. Remember, your brain is most useful to you when used in service of your heart. Heart-centered practices bring your awareness to your heart so it can guide you. These practices can also help you develop greater self-compassion and gentleness. Practice empathy, putting yourself in others' shoes, and connection through relationships. Follow the path of the Beauty Way, which is the way of love and light.

Another way to activate and engage the right brain is to create new experiences. Travel to a new place, cook a new recipe, try a new art project or meditation practice. Laughter and humor also arise from the right brain, so use your funny bone! As you can see, the ways you can develop your right brain capacity are extensive, and all are beneficial. As you activate your right brain more fully, you will begin to notice an internal feeling of balance and joy. Natural psychic ability, flow, and synchronicity will happen in your life. You will notice your living connection and relationship to life. You will be more present fully in each moment, and your life will take on a beauty and aliveness like never before. You will exist in the realm of your heart. You will experience your true nature, the freedom and perfection of your divine blueprint. The more you enable your right brain, the more you will abide in deep joy and fulfillment.

The divine feminine is here to rise to her rightful place and to bring balance and care to the suffering Earth. She will help the world remember what the divine masculine looks like, and how these two powers work together so beautifully. We are holders of the balance medicine, and although we have primarily focused on the feminine right brain in this message, we acknowledge the importance of the left brain divine masculine as well. The divine masculine understands its role as guardian, activator, and leader for the benefit of all life. The divine masculine holds the energies of determination, movement, strength, action, and nobility. You can access all of these qualities through healing your divine masculine aspects.

In our journey, we will offer you a healing ceremony designed to bring your divine feminine and divine masculine energies into balance. It will also help activate your right brain, heart, and energy flow in your spine.

Practices to Help You Align and Balance

- Work with sound current for vibrational healing through music, toning, singing, and crystal bowls. This will bring your body into higher realm resonance.
- Use the Scroll of Divine Alignment to anchor the new flow and brain balance within you.
- Pursue creative outlets that make your soul sing.
- Create through art, photography, cooking, singing, dancing, adventures, and other arts.
- Participate in yoga, Pilates, martial arts, or other dharmas to balance the energy within your form.
- Receive healing energy treatments like massage, cranio-sacral work, and other energy healing modalities regularly.
- Limit your screen time and disconnect from modern media. Balance times when you need to be online with equal or more time in Nature.
- Do something new every day.
- Plan activities that charge your energy; avoid ones that deplete it.
- Practice resting in both your divine feminine and divine masculine energies, intending to balance your inner self.
- Prioritize the development of right-brain living.
- Connect with the indigo ray color in your life, making your intention for alignment conscious and clear.
- Learn more about your divine masculine energy and how to cultivate it in your life. Work to heal unhealthy masculine patterns within.
- Cultivate your divine feminine energy in all ways that speak to you.

Grandmother Izoma and Grandfather Skylan Guided Alignment Journey

The Prayer of Stella Maris

Divine Maha Ocean Mother:

Hold me in your warm embrace,
Float me in your cosmic ocean of grace.
Refresh me with your "I AM" presence,
Bless my waters with divine light and self-realization.
Weightless and suspended in light,
Wave after wave of divine love flows through my multidimensional form.
Vitality, health, and renewal restores me to my true self.
Receiving the light of the Divine Feminine.
Receiving the light of the Divine Masculine.
Healing balance within and without.
All parts of myself deeply loved.
No sound or movement, resting in your Oneness,
Great Mother of All of Life,
I remember who I am.
A starlight being, a beautiful creation of stardust and divine water light.
Living Divinity.
Surrounded by my divine family, I imagine the possible for all of life.
Returning to oneness,
I bless myself.
I love myself.
I know myself.
I am free.
I am my true self forevermore.

Let us begin:

I place my hand on my heart and take three deep breaths. I am on the beach, listening to the sound of waves lapping against the shore. It is night, and the scent of the seawater flows through my hair. A thousand stars twinkle above me, sending sparkling messages of love. I am in awe of the mystery of life as I witness the unspeakable beauty of the night sky. The ocean ripples as Grandmother Izoma and Grandfather Skylan rise before me. Grandmother is dark gray, with sacred geometric symbols marking her body. Grandfather is a pinkish gray, with light language symbols etched along his back. He greets me with wise and kind eyes.

The warm water greets my body as I dive into the sea. The elders invite me to place my arms around their dorsal fins, and they pull me quickly out into the open ocean. The ride is exhilarating, and I am filled with total faith in their guidance. We pause to watch a crescent yellow moon slowly rise on the horizon. The moonlight nourishes my skin and body with its luminescence. I soak in the light.

I lie back, allowing the ocean saltwater to float me on the surface, with my ears just under water. Grandmother and grandfather slowly swim around me, turning my body in a clockwise direction. Then they switch direction, spinning me slowly to the left. I enjoy the sensation of being moved by the currents. Shooting stars create patterns across the sky. Izoma pushes her rostrum (nose) against the top of my head. The pressure against my crown chakra fills my head with purple-blue light. Grandfather Skylan presses his rostrum on the soles of my feet. An indigo ray descends from the top of my head and ascends from my feet, meeting in the middle of my body and exploding like fireworks down my spine. The indigo light changes to silver and then white. I hear Izoma speak:

"Your right and left hemispheres are now in perfect alignment with your heart. Your divine masculine and divine feminine energies are balanced. Your brain physiology is now available in service to your Higher Self. It is free from past conditioning, beliefs, and thoughts. Balance and equanimity exist within your form once more. Discover the peace that comes with divine alignment."

I slowly open my eyes. The silver-white stars are so close I can almost touch them. The moonlight and starlight swirl together, creating a dome around my body. The light encircles me as I drink it with thirst. The elders begin to sing and click, creating light language symbols that land on my body. These symbols activate new intelligence, alignment, and abilities. The beautiful dolphin sounds infuse my energy field. Then it is quiet, and the elders gently nudge me to move upright. As they glide me through the water toward the shore, I thank them for their blessings. They disappear into the night. I walk out of the water, finding a scroll in my hand. I unroll it and read aloud:

The Scroll of Divine Alignment

Standing in the power and peace of my divinity, I proclaim:

I exist in divine alignment

I receive the blessing of the indigo ray

My balance creates peace and harmony within my form

My inner divine masculine and divine feminine work together
in peace and partnership

Each aspect is honored and adored

My right and left brain are in balance

I engage in right-brain activities daily to create more balance
and to free myself from the left-brain-dominant world

My balanced brain brings me expanded capabilities
and positively impacts all life

My brain works in service to my heart

I honor my inner divine masculine and inner divine feminine

My balance allows more of my Higher Self to exist within my form

Moonlight and starlight bless my body with their mystic light

I receive light language symbols that anchor my new way of being

In perfect balance, I rest in my divinity

My divinity connects me with the oneness of all beings

Chapter 18
Kelti
Messenger of Divine Freedom

Kelti Speaks:

I am Kelti, an adolescent male in the pod of Stella Maris. I offer you the blessing of the red ray to activate your awakening, independence, authenticity, and freedom. I will assist you in breaking free from old paradigms and with embracing your original and authentic self. This freedom requires the dissolution of what is no longer working in your life. The spirit of rebellion can be invoked to help you break free. I live as a true rebel! Liberation means healing your old ways of living, and awakening to the new. Are you ready for divine freedom?

My Message for You

You are going through the early stages of awakening. What has motivated you in the past no longer works, and you can see the craziness of your modern life. You may feel isolated from others who are still living in the old way, for they do not understand your discontent. You exist between two worlds, no longer run by your ego, but not yet fully awake and operating as your Higher Self. Arising in two realities, it is normal to feel uncomfortable, like you are split between two worlds.

Divine awakening is a conscious choice to stand as your Higher Self in every moment. Awakening can happen instantly or seemingly take linear time. Waking up is not easy, but it is absolutely worth it, so don't give up. The metaphor of waking up in the morning is a good way to explain the process to you. You are comfortable and cozy in your warm bed—until your alarm goes off. *Beep, beep, beep!* The loud sound wakes you up and demands you start your day. Sometimes you don't want to get up, and you might throw the alarm across the room and hide under the blankets.

The process of awakening is just like this, especially when you are here to live your divine purpose. The freedom alarm is loud and annoying and never goes away . . . ever. Your heart will not give you peace and is not content to "be quiet." Its calling can make you feel agitated and angry, but know it is your highest self calling you to your destiny. Rise, answer the call, and meet your highest freedom.

Buried in your heart is the possibility of an awakened life. You can feel the potential in your bones. Liberation and freedom usually come with the disruption of your normal life. Consent to this great upheaval, knowing it will free you in the end. Use your anger constructively to break free from viral belief systems and cultural constructs that are no longer of use to you. Anger is a true gift because it calls you into action, motivates and energizes, and emboldens you until you are free. Embrace your feelings of anger—for they show you that you are on the right track.

Refuse to be controlled and manipulated by outside influences that do not have your best interests in mind. Remember not to label your refusal to participate in outdated constructs as a problem, illness, or issue. This new choice is actually the solution. Be courageous in your resolve, committing to your liberation and the freedom of all beings.

You possess a creative brilliance like no other. Embrace your originality. Walk your own walk, talk your own talk. Be a rebel within the matrix. Reject anything that is not aligned with you. Express yourself artistically, creatively, and originally, and please have a great time doing it.

Choose freedom by being your freaking awesome shining-star self, independent and unapologetic, following the guidance of your fabulous heart. Take the greatest adventure of your life and see what is on the other side. You will rock this world. You will be an explosion of light. Enter the dark places within you, shining the light of your Higher Self to transform it all. Trust your own inner guidance system. Trust your divine blueprint, and know you are here to live an extraordinary purpose. A life like no other. Trust life again, and forget what anyone else thinks. Stay focused and committed to yourself every day.

Be a lightning bolt for others, who will see your strength and ability to live outside of the box. You will become an inspiration, a force of Nature leading others to a new way of being. If they can receive your blessing, you will change their world. Do not be surprised if some people can't handle the heat. Deeply respect their path, and move on with yours.

Connect with others who resonate with you. Find your soul friends, and hang out together. Stepping into your Higher Self will magnetize new friends into your life. Brainstorm together new out-of-the-box ideas, and lift each other up. Co-create new constructs and paradigms. Design it all anew with the divine blueprints of your collective souls. Take a stand for all those who are ready to break free, and work together to change what needs changing.

My words are the alarm you have been waiting for, so WAKE UP! Rub your eyes, have a stretch, and get busy being the authentic you. It is time!!!

Practices to Support Your Freedom

- Mind your business, and understand what is not your business.
- Take a break from world news.
- Embrace your anger as a powerful liberator and a valid feeling. Release excess anger through physical outlets.
- Set the intention to awaken in your life.
- Allow discontent to guide you to freedom.
- Be unique, and follow your divine blueprint.
- Use the word "no" when needed and "yes" when needed.
- Soar on the wings of your divine freedom.
- Embrace your originality.
- Free yourself from what "everybody else" thinks.
- Dare greatly.
- Find your tribe, and engage in purposeful action.
- Be a part of movements that awaken others.
- Connect with the red ray color in your life through the color red. Set your intention for divine freedom and liberation.
- Work with the Divine Scroll of Liberation daily.

Kelti Divine Freedom Activation

The Prayer of Stella Maris

Divine Maha Ocean Mother:

Hold me in your warm embrace,
Float me in your cosmic ocean of grace.
Refresh me with your "I AM" presence,
Bless my waters with divine light and self-realization.
Weightless and suspended in light,
Wave after wave of divine love flows through my multidimensional form.
Vitality, health, and renewal restores me to my true self.
Receiving the light of the Divine Feminine.
Receiving the light of the Divine Masculine.
Healing balance within and without.
All parts of myself deeply loved.
No sound or movement, resting in your Oneness,
Great Mother of All of Life,
I remember who I am.
A starlight being, a beautiful creation of stardust and divine water light.
Living Divinity.
Surrounded by my divine family, I imagine the possible for all of life.
Returning to oneness,
I bless myself.
I love myself.
I know myself.
I am free.
I am my true self forevermore.

Let us begin:

I place my hand on my heart and take three deep breaths. I am standing on a great cliff overlooking the ocean. The wind whips through my hair, billowing my white robe. A storm brews, revealing funnel clouds and lightning in the distance. Light rain falls on my face, feeling warm and refreshing. Gazing at the sea, I notice the shape of a lone dolphin swimming toward me. He is light gray, with a triangle shape on his dorsal fin. As he reaches the rocky shore, he speeds up, leaping out of the ocean and transforming into a white and gray eagle. He soars on the currents of the wind, higher and higher. He lands next to me with a great whoosh, transforming into a teen boy with gray eyes and sandy brown hair. "Hey," he says, "I'm Kelti." I greet him with a wide smile, as a gust of wind blows us closer together.

"Would you like to join me for an adventure?" he asks. I nod my head yes.

"Let's have a chat first." A spark of lightning and the sound of rolling thunder fills the air. "This adventure will take great courage. . . . My hope is that you will feel stronger after you face your fears. You have great inner strength and simply need to remember." Another gust of wind blows against me, pushing me backward. I steady myself by sliding my foot under a nearby rock.

"Do you know that the wind is the only element on Earth that is invisible?" Kelti continues. "You can't see it, yet you can feel its presence and strength as it meets your form. The wind is there, but remains elusive to your sight. The same is true of the invisible realm of the Higher Self. You can only know yourself through direct experience and if you are willing to dive into the unknown. I invite you to have faith in the existence of things that you can't see. This faith will bring you freedom and will awaken your Higher Self, life purpose, brilliance, and originality. I invite you to see with your spiritual senses and to develop unbreakable faith in yourself and in the support of the universe.

"Within the invisible realms reside your guides, angels, the ascended masters, and other helpful beings. Just beyond the visible light waves are the infrared, the ultraviolet, and beyond. This is where we exist; we are real, and we are here. You know this is true; ask your heart! We are here to assist with your liberation and freedom. Are you ready to be free? Shall we take a leap of faith?"

"Yes," I reply.

Kelti transforms into a white eagle, rising off the ground as the wind blows through his great wings. He carefully lands on my right shoulder, wrapping his talons gently for balance. Using his beak, he gently taps the top of my head, and I feel my body changing. Great white wings emerge from my back, flapping in the wind. My wings are about twice my height, and I happily realize I am an angel! I am surprised how natural my angelic form feels. The wind blows through my white feathers as I lift off of the ground.

Kelti flies toward the cliff, communicating telepathically that we will jump off together. Fear pulses through my body as I hover, frozen, peering over the edge. The ocean crashes angrily against the rocks. The cliff is at least five hundred feet high, and I wonder how many seconds it will take for me to hit the jagged stones. Lightning strikes loud and fierce, shaking my nerves to the core. I don't know if my wings will work. Can I really fly? Or is this the end of my existence? A small rock dislodges from the cliff and falls silently toward the ocean below.

I lock eyes with Kelti, and we leap off the edge. My eyes are shut tight; my body tense as it anticipates its fatal crash against the rocks. I wait, breathless. Nothing happens. I open my eyes, realizing I am soaring over the ocean, Kelti at my side. We are flying through an epic storm, filled with dark clouds and roaring wind. Lightning strikes around us, as the raw power of electricity is revealed. I am exhilarated by the discovery that my wings know how to fly on their own. They guide me effortlessly through the clouds and lightning. Bolts create brilliant fireworks of red, violet, white, and gold light that reflect against the clouds.

I have never been this close to a storm, let alone in the middle of one, and the raw power and intensity is incredible. I match the intensity, shouting at the top of my lungs. Kelti encourages me to shout more, and my voice releases all of my pent-up feelings, especially rage and anger. Screaming like a banshee, I liberate years of angry emotions. My imprisoned feelings fly out of my throat, riding upon the wind to freedom. Free at last! I witness some feelings have a unique expression of form and color. Some sprout wings and fly away like dragonflies. The storm calms and the clouds dissipate, revealing a bright blue sky. Kelti and I soar in circles over the calm ocean, cutting through the air with our aerodynamic wings.

We land back on the cliffs, touching the tips of our wings together one last time. "Thank you," I say. He nods with a sparkling smirk and dives off the cliff, changing back into a dolphin. I notice a scroll in my hand. I unfold it and read aloud:

The Scroll of Divine Freedom

Standing in the power and peace of my divinity, I proclaim:

I am free, I am freedom, I am liberated

I leap into my highest destiny

I am an original, never to be created again

I embrace my anger and deepest feelings, honoring them with expression

My feelings offer me divine guidance, and as I set them free
I hear their messages clearly

I don't care what anyone else thinks

I use my inner rebel to break free from past beliefs
and negative cultural conditioning

My anger energizes me to take action for my Higher Self

In facing my fears, I discover my courage

I trust in my Higher Self and invisible support team

I am supported by the wind of creation

My spiritual senses operate my awareness

I exist as my authentic and true self

I am comfortable living outside the box!

I inspire others to break free

I choose an awakened life

I know how to fly, I fly on my angelic wings of faith and trust

Without knowing where, without knowing why, I leap, I love, I fly

Chapter 19
Queen A'Mara

Queen A'Mara Speaks:

I am Queen Krystala A'Mara, priestess of the ocean and guide of Stella Maris. I reside on the planet of Hydras in the Pleiades star system, where I tend to the temple of Stella Maris. My title of queen reflects my royalty, sovereignty, and nobility. The name Krystala reflects my unity with divine feminine Christ consciousness. My name A'Mara means beloved heart, immortal, and eternal beauty. It is an expression of the pure radiance of my crystalline diamond essence. I bless you with the blue ray of nobility. Welcome to my domain of water light. Here you will receive more of your true self. Receive the blessings of your spiral heart, dear one. Aka lan jai—at heart, we are one.

I appear to you now in the form of a beautiful woman, radiating white and silver light. Let me describe myself to you. My flowing aqua-blue hair cascades down my back, highlighting my electric-blue eyes. My eyes change color according to my emotions: sometimes they are green, violet, or purple. The same is true of my clothing. I adorn myself in different fashions and colors through the power of my intention. It is quite fun! Today, I am wearing a gold crown, encrusted with blue and purple crystals that hold unique healing power. There are topazes, lapises, and sapphires. One clear blue teardrop of topaz rests upon my forehead.

A brilliant white dress billows and flows around my body, dancing with a life of its own. My neck is adorned with a crystal necklace, with one shining white stone which rests on my chest. The symbol of the sacred spiral is permanently etched over my heart. I have similar smaller spirals on the bottoms of my feet and palms of my hands.

Transcending any perception of separateness, my awareness is enlightened or awake. I call this consciousness illumined. Illumination is resting in the heart of the Source and knowing yourself as the light of the Divine Mother. This illumined awareness is given freely to all by grace. You are always free to truly experience your luminosity or brightness, standing in full recognition of your Higher Self.

My Message for You

You are a being of the light and so you share all of my divine qualities. I am here to bless you with remembrance of your divine nobility. You are royal. You are noble. You are free. You are sovereign. Let me help you remember yourself as a king or queen of the one true heart.

Breathing liquid light, I rest in the Source of oneness. From time to time, aspects of my Higher Self descend like shooting stars in order to offer my help in many places. My deep compassion moves me to go on missions where there is suffering. I am multidimensional, existing both here and elsewhere simultaneously. How is it possible to exist in more than one world simultaneously? What a great and divine mystery! The mystery of my existence and yours.

The Temple of Stella Maris

Through the seas of time and space, my Higher Self remains in Hydras, a planet orbiting the Pleiadian star Maya. Our planet's surface is made entirely of water. We have vast oceans, with crystal cities built above and below the water's surface. Our beautiful homes have elaborate gardens and stunning landscapes. We even have mountains under the sea! The beauty of Hydras often takes my breath away. The Stella Maris crystalline temple floats on the Dritan Sea. The Stella Maris dolphins often reside here with me, returning to our temple whenever they choose. You have now met many of them—Theseus, Mahadra, Kaleosi, Drahana, Kelti, Luz, Ama, Phaedra, Lolli, Ra, and Izoma and Skylan.

Stella Maris Speaks

The Stella Maris council was created through our shared vision for galactic peace. Mother Mary, Quan Yin, Stella Maris, and myself have been part of the council from its inception. The intention of the council is to serve the illumination and awakening of all beings. It is my greatest honor to serve in this way. The Stella Maris temple was specifically built to harness and project healing waves of light, and its very structure holds energetic resonance and transmission. In this sacred place, we hold collective intentions and healing prayers for the awakening of other worlds. We regularly do healing ceremonies, activating our highest prayers with sound and light. We create beautiful prayers for you here.

I spend my days serving the temple. I am often seated on a throne of clear quartz, where I gaze at a large round pool of water that stands at the center of the temple. Thousands of flowers bloom here, especially lotuses and roses. Roses of every color imaginable climb up the walls, emanating the sweet fragrance of love. Lotus flowers bloom within the water, with pink and yellow centers. Oh, yes, I must tell you about the orchids; we have every color, and I especially love the violet ones.

The sound of flowing water fills the temple from all directions. Through the clear crystal ceiling, I have a wonderful view of the sky, full of the stars and our two golden moons. Hydras has extraordinary views of the cosmos. The dolphins usually enter the temple through the bottom, where there are four doorways. All council members gather around the central pool. The dolphins usually choose to remain in the water for our meetings (unless they change form). When we meet, we discuss our current missions, participate in ceremony, and create living prayers.

The experience of color and light is more vibrant in Hydras. Energy waves are visible, and our bodies exist in less density in the higher realms. In my form here, I do not experience pain or sickness. We have unlimited creativity, instantly manifesting anything through our intentions. We are true Imagineers of our reality, planting seeds of creation. Yes, we live in a place where divine magic is very much alive and used daily.

As I describe my life here, you may have memories surface of living somewhere like this. Many Starseed light activators come from such places. On Hydras, we live in harmony, and all beings are loved, respected, and honored. We recognize the divinity within all of life. Individual and collective needs are met effortlessly, with no need to struggle. We have a peaceful community and work together as co-creators and friends. All is very, very well here. From our place of peace, we send blessings to other worlds for their evolution. We freely share our knowledge of how to exist in this harmonious way. I hope my description of life on Hydras inspires you and helps you remember what is possible. Your light work on Earth is deeply honored here, and I acknowledge the courage it takes for you volunteer on Earth.

Remember, you are on Gaia Earth to bring balance through the light of your true self. You are safe. You are not lost. You are strong. Your Higher Self remains firmly seated in the divine and can always offer you guidance from the light domains.

Practices for Remembering Your Divine Nobility

- Make yourself a crown!
- Connect through your imagination to the realms of light and other star nations.
- Honor yourself through impeccable self-care and self-love.
- Wear clothing that makes your heart sing. Adorn your beautiful form with jewelry or symbols that speak to you.
- Create a temple or sacred environment where you can feel your Holy Self.
- Have faith in what is beyond your human comprehension.
- Use the power of your voice to speak affirmations that proclaim your divinity, nobility, and royalty.
- Connect to the stars at night, breathing in the awe and joy they bring to your heart.
- Access the blue ray through your imagination, food, clothing, and environment.
- Use the Scroll of Divine Nobility to activate your royalty consciousness daily. This will raise your self-confidence and self-remembrance.

Queen A'Mara
Divine Nobility Visionary Journey

The Prayer of Stella Maris

Divine Maha Ocean Mother:

Hold me in your warm embrace,
Float me in your cosmic ocean of grace.
Refresh me with your "I AM" presence,
Bless my waters with divine light and self-realization.
Weightless and suspended in light,
Wave after wave of divine love flows through my multidimensional form.
Vitality, health, and renewal restores me to my true self.
Receiving the light of the Divine Feminine.
Receiving the light of the Divine Masculine.
Healing balance within and without.
All parts of myself deeply loved.
No sound or movement, resting in your Oneness,
Great Mother of All of Life,
I remember who I am.
A starlight being, a beautiful creation of stardust and divine water light.
Living Divinity.
Surrounded by my divine family, I imagine the possible for all of life.
Returning to oneness,
I bless myself.
I love myself.
I know myself.
I am free.
I am my true self forevermore.

Let us begin:

I bring my hand to my heart and take three deep breaths. I am standing on a white-sand beach near the bright, aqua sea. The sound of waves echoes through my ears. I breathe in the scent of jasmine, which infuses me with a calm peacefulness. My toes dig into the sand, creating a crunching sound. I raise my arms to the sky in reverence and deep gratitude for the divine help that is always available to me. I rest my hands on my heart in prayer.

They are coming with the sound of moving water, sonar clicks, and quiet singing. The members of Stella Maris rise up and greet me with huge smiles. On the left are Theseus, Mahadra, and Kaleosi. On the right, Izoma, Skylan, Kelti, and Drahana. Directly in front of me are Luz, Ra, Lolli, Ama, and Phaedra. They communicate telepathically, "Beloved! We are so happy to see you! Come, let's go on a journey together; we will take you home."

I wade into the sea and swim toward them. Quickly transforming into my dolphin form, I glide effortlessly through the water. We swim toward a blue doorway at the bottom of the ocean. We swim through and come out the other side, bathed in starlight.

We are floating in the vast ocean of space, dark blackness and sparkling starlight. We move effortlessly, catching invisible dark waves. I leap and jump through the peaceful sacred space, gliding to the sound of pure stillness. The stars of the seven sisters shine brightly before me, singing a homecoming melody.

An overwhelming feeling of sadness overtakes me, causing tears to stream down my face. I have missed this place so much. Distant memories pass before my eyes, confirming this is one of my soul homes. Tears drip off my face, taking flight into space like small diamonds. My tears create beautiful water tapestries, as I receive the healing of my own pure water medicine. I feel held by the black no-thingness all around me, the Divine Mother.

As we get closer, my excitement grows. The seven stars glow with a bluish-white light, pulsing a welcome message. Stella Maris turns toward the right, and I hear the word "Maya" within my mind. A bright, golden star shines brilliantly before me, and I glide close, taking in its appearance. Nestled below Maya, I see a bright blue planet . . . Hydras. I remember this place. Descending into the atmosphere with anticipation, I dip and dive, my stomach leaping with butterflies. Flying over the expansive oceans of deep blue, aqua, and green, I take in the sight of crystal cities and underwater mountains. The Stella Maris dolphins are with me, laughing, as we use our invisible wings to soar over the expansive water.

A great crystal temple appears, floating on the sea. The main building is a large glass dome made out of iridescent crystal. I follow Stella Maris as they dive into the water, entering the temple through a rainbow doorway at its base. We arise in a circular pool in the center of the temple. Seated around us on majestic thrones are Mother Mary, Queen A'Mara, and Quan Yin. The thrones create a trinity or triangle inside the temple. The divine feminine masters each wear beautiful flowing dresses. Smiling lovingly, they welcome us to the temple of Stella Maris in unison. Mother Mary's throne is adorned with roses that cascade around her in all directions. They bloom in full glory, miraculously without thorns. Mother Mary wears a crown of rose quartz on her beautiful head and a light pink dress. Queen A'Mara sits nearby on a clear crystalline throne, her bright blue hair flowing around her face. She wears a capiz-shell crown with a large blue crystal dangling over her third eye. Her throne is adorned with crystals and sea shells. Water flows beneath her seat, changing color from blue to green. Quan Yin rests upon a golden throne with a pink lotus base. She is wearing a white robe and a gold crown with rainbow diamonds. Rainbow reflections cast light around her throne and throughout the temple.

The three divine feminine masters motion for me to ascend the crystal steps. I realize I am now in my human form and walk up the steps easily, instantly dried by a warm breeze of gardenia and jasmine. I am wearing a flowing white gown. Additional members of Stella Maris arrive in the temple with a series of splashes and jumps. They swim around happily and then become still, observing us sweetly.

There is a crystal throne for me, one of the most beautiful I have ever seen. It is made of blooming white flowers: white roses, jasmine, gardenia, hydrangea, and lotus. All three divine feminine masters motion toward the throne, inviting me to take my seat. I am honored and feel like royalty. Dropping instantly into a state of deep relaxation, I sit proudly. My eyes become heavy, and I close them. I meditate to the sound of flowing water, feeling the sensation of a gentle breeze upon my face. My heart is as wide as the sky, and I feel happy, like a thousand butterflies have broken free from my chrysalis chest. The light in the temple is pure white and descends gently through the top of my head. It moves down my spine, all the way to the tips of my toes. Every cell in my body feels recharged, healed, and energized.

19: Queen A'Mara

Someone touches my feet, and I open my eyes. The three divine feminine masters are bowing before me, placing their hands on my feet. I am surprised by the honor they are showing me. Behind them, in the pool, the dolphins watch me in rapt attention, as the masters begin to sing a beautiful and lilting song. I recognize the tune. It is a song that tugs at my memory. Quan Yin places her hands on my heart, Queen A'Mara places her hands on the top of my head, and Mother Mary holds my feet. I witness rays of light—white, rainbow, pink, and blue—emanating from their hands and entering my body. They whisper softly in unison:

"Beloved, you are created in the image and likeness of the one true heart, the Divine Mother herself. You are light and love in human form. You deserve great honor. We now restore the memory of your true Higher Self. You are divine. You are royal. You are holy. You can now fly in the freedom of your sovereignty. You are of noble birth, and we deeply honor you as our beloved friend, our beloved queen, our beloved heart."

Mother Mary places a starlight crown upon my head. Silver with bright shining stars, a single glowing star dangles over my forehead. I feel my essence as a starlight water being. My body begins to glow as it morphs into a five-pointed star shining with brilliant light. Quan Yin anoints me with sacred water, and Queen A'Mara presses lotus oil on my forehead.

The divine feminine masters stand before me. I bow to them in reverence, my heart breaking from their unspeakable grace. I lean forward and prostrate on the ground in a puddle of joy. I am encircled by millions of invisible arms, which lift me back on my feet. Standing eye to eye in a circle with Queen A'Mara, Quan Yin, and Mother Mary, we hold hands, gazing at each other with love.

The dolphins of Stella Maris twirl in the air, splashing the water in celebration! I hug my beautiful divine masters once more and then leap off into the pool, feeling my dolphin form return. Stella Maris surrounds me in a vortex of water light. I jump high, creating spirals and infinity signs in the air. I flow in a circle with my dear friends. I realize the profound activations and initiations I have received in the temple. This experience will be forever imprinted within my heart.

We dive deep to exit the temple, and lift into the night sky. We break through the atmosphere, returning to the vast dark space. Gaia Earth comes into view, and I marvel at her beauty, knowing clearly my heart's desire to heal her. I float among the stars for a final moment with Stella Maris, feeling overwhelming gratitude. Tears of joy stream down my face, as we swirl together in a loving embrace. My eyes shine with new awareness and vision.

I arrive back on the white-sand beach and watch as the fins of Stella Maris disappear on the horizon. I know we will meet again, and this makes my heart sing. I notice a scroll in my right hand, unfold it, and read aloud:

The Scroll of Divine Nobility

Standing in the power and peace of my divinity, I proclaim:

I am divine

I am noble

I am royal

I am a queen, a king, a being of unity consciousness

I am sovereign and free

I honor my own being and all of life

I am created in the image and likeness of the Divine Mother

I am the one true heart of all existence

I remember my divine self

I reclaim my ancient wisdom

I treat myself with reverence and respect
knowing that I have a great divine purpose

I bring forth my soul's wisdom from all of my lifetimes

I am a Starseed light activator

My form is created from stardust and water light

I am a beautiful shooting star

I accept my crown as a symbol of my nobility and royalty

I lead others through the guidance of my pure heart and soul light

My life is a gift to the world

Chapter 20
Drahana
Messenger of Earth Wisdom

Drahana Speaks:

My name is Drahana, and it means "precious," a word that signifies my devotion to the sanctity of all life. I am an adolescent girl and a messenger of Earth wisdom. I bless you with the green ray of Earth leadership so you can become a light warrior for Gaia Earth and all of her creatures. Trained as a priestess of the Divine Mother, I am part of an unbroken lineage of divine feminine leaders who work to restore balance.

My Message for You

You are a precious being. You appear to be in physical form, but are actually crystalline water light. You arc a unique creation of the Divine Mother. You are a beautiful fractal, a sacred geometric shape, with infinite complexity and evolving self-awareness.

There has been a renewed interest in ancient societies in your modern world. Past cultures model a way of life with balance and unity. Messengers from ancient cultures, such as myself, are here to guide you so you can return to this way of life. You also may have lived in these societies and carry wisdom that can benefit the world. Thank you for stepping into your leadership and making your greatest offering.

As we have explained, you have been given immense creative power as part of your divine inheritance. Use your power wisely, with the knowledge that you are here to create a new Earth. You are literally activating the light of your soul here to create a new world.

Lemuria

The civilization of Lemuria existed on a large continent in the Pacific Ocean for thousands of years. After a cataclysmic earthly event, the entire continent disappeared into the ocean, creating great trauma and loss of life. After the physical destruction of Lemuria, many of the beings who lived there shifted into higher dimensional realities. This is why I sometimes speak of Lemuria in the present tense—it still remains in many ways. Lemuria is sometimes referred to as Mu, the motherland. The beings of Lemuria are highly evolved and spiritual. Many of these advanced souls have reincarnated on Earth during this time of awakening, to help as light activators.

Let's travel together to ancient Lemuria. Imagine a vibrant place of beauty. The energy here is fluid, and your Higher Self is able to create without limitation, manifesting your intentions easily into form. The Lemurians know how to live in alignment with the divine feminine and divine masculine. They embrace the Beauty Way, which embodies reverence, respect, and love for all beings. Lemuria is sometimes called Mu, which means "pure motherland." Lemurians honor all of life as sacred and understand all beings are family. There is no hierarchy, only a circle of connection. All beings are encouraged to follow their heart's calling and to live their purpose. Lemurians are born magicians, able to create from the power of their imagination and intention. They are masters of co-creation with the Divine Mother, and work with the power of their Higher Self divine magic. In our temples, they easily access the higher realms as a resource. Lemurians also connect with the natural forces on Earth, communicating with other planets, animals, and stones. We understand the healing powers of our Solstar allies.

Lemuria is an ocean-based culture where people relate to water as a living being. The ocean is respected as the physical form of the Divine Mother. There are sacred orders and high councils devoted solely to water blessing and healing. The healing water energy of Lemuria still exists on your Earth in certain Earth locations, such as the islands of Kauai and Bali.

The Indigenous People of the Earth Will Lead You

The Lemurian way of life exists today in many indigenous Earth cultures. These cultures have endured incredible hardship. Even with all of their challenges, they rise again and again, offering leadership through their teachings. Honor their wisdom, and ask with humility for them to teach you.

The indigenous people of Gaia Earth are great leaders who are here to assist you. These incredible light workers have carried wisdom forward for hundreds of generations, never losing their connection with the Divine Mother, even under the most horrific and brutal experiences. Take responsibility, and make amends for what has occurred in the past. Remedy past injustices, and move forward in unity with your brothers and sisters. Empower them to lead you, for they know the returning way, how to move back into right alignment with Gaia Earth. Create leadership alliances and rise together. Support the indigenous peoples' missions in all ways. Honor and bless them. Listen to their guidance. Work together to restore what has been broken. Restore the sacred balance. You have a great deal to learn about living in balance.

Gaia Earth has sustained herself through her beautiful designs for millions of years. Many of the answers you seek are already here, just waiting for you to discover them. Gaia Earth has perfectly designed systems throughout Nature. Observe the solutions that are revealed all around you. Unify your consciousness and ask questions to Nature with great care. You will find the solutions you seek in the natural world.

Practices for Integrating Earth Wisdom

- Go outside!
- Immerse yourself in the majesty and magnificence of Gaia Earth.
- Connect with animals, plants, and other sentient beings. Listen to their voices and messages.
- Support indigenous people, helping them to heal through your love and recognition of their incredible gifts. Assist them in rising to positions of leadership so they can share their wisdom.
- Mentor or study with indigenous people.
- Learn more about animal symbolism, and understand the messages you receive daily.
- Learn more about ancient cultures and places such as Lemuria.
- Participate in warrior practices that build your strength and light.
- Value connection, and understand the way natural systems work on Gaia Earth.
- Align your life with your values and integrity.
- Engage in a living relationship with water every day.
- Travel to sacred locations to bring your blessings, and receive infinitely the blessings of the magic they hold.
- Gather in community to honor the Source, and work together to change and balance the world.
- Call on and receive the support of Stella Maris and other Solstar light activators.
- Connect with the green ray in your life. Go outdoors and invoke its power to recharge and enliven you as a warrior of the light.
- Use the Scroll of Light Leadership to anchor your presence as a leader of peace and balance on Earth.

Drahana Light Warrior Activation

The Prayer of Stella Maris

Divine Maha Ocean Mother:

Hold me in your warm embrace,
Float me in your cosmic ocean of grace.
Refresh me with your "I AM" presence,
Bless my waters with divine light and self-realization.
Weightless and suspended in light,
Wave after wave of divine love flows through my multidimensional form.
Vitality, health, and renewal restores me to my true self.
Receiving the light of the Divine Feminine.
Receiving the light of the Divine Masculine.
Healing balance within and without.
All parts of myself deeply loved.
No sound or movement, resting in your Oneness,
Great Mother of All of Life,
I remember who I am.
A starlight being, a beautiful creation of stardust and divine water light.
Living Divinity.
Surrounded by my divine family, I imagine the possible for all of life.
Returning to oneness,
I bless myself.
I love myself.
I know myself.
I am free.
I am my true self forevermore.

Let us begin:

I place my hand on my heart and take three deep breaths. A sense of completion flows through me. The sound of playing dolphins dances through my ears, and I slowly open my eyes. I am standing on a grassy green overlook, gazing at the deep blue sea. A brilliant rainbow shines down from the clouds, diving into the water and disappearing. In front of the enormous rainbow is the pod of Stella Maris, who play together in joyful radiance.

I am honored to know they are always here, blessing me from the higher realms. Light messenger friends who model profound unity and connection to the ineffable mystery of the Divine Mother.

Drahana comes forward, inviting me to join her. She is dark gray, with a wing symbol across her forehead. I dive off the overlook without a thought, trusting my wings will emerge. Drahana rises to meet me, changing into her angelic form. We meet in the air with a rush of wings, and begin soaring over the vistas of an ancient land. I see green volcanic mountains rising steeply out of the ocean. There are lush forests and waterfalls. White birds fly below us and land in the tops of flowering orange trees.

We land at the base of a mountain near a waterfall. Sacred stones rest firmly upon the bright green grass. At the base of the waterfall there is a deep indigo pool. Behind the waterfall, I can see a cave, hidden from view. Indigenous shamans all dressed in white emerge from the cave. They gather in a circle around the pool, holding hands to signal the beginning of a ceremony. We join the circle, standing close to the water's edge. My bare feet delight in the softness of the fresh grass. A breeze brings the scent of tropical flowers. One of the shamans steps forward, beginning the ceremony with an invocation. She speaks to the water first, honoring it, this conscious being. Being here is the answer to my prayers. I am blessed, I am grateful. All my life, I have been waiting for this moment of initiation.

Water rises from the pool, molding itself into different shapes, expressing its aliveness and freedom of movement. It becomes a large glowing orb. The orb hovers about twenty feet over our heads, growing larger and more full. Tiny water droplets float from the orb suspended in the air. The droplets move out in all directions, landing on my face with the gentle touch of a mother's kiss. More drops land on my body, anointing me with living water. I hear the water say, "I love you, I bless you!"

The water falls back into the pool with a great splash, and we stand in a white mist. A shaman recites a blessing, and the sound of drumming begins.

An elder shaman steps forward. He has red and black symbols painted onto his face. He wears a red beaded necklace. Elaborate black symbols are painted on his arms and legs. He holds a peace pipe. The sky darkens into night; a thousand stars shine above, listening with bated breath to his every word. He invites the ancestors, the star people, and the Creator to join our circle. He calls in the four directions, and instantaneously four fires light around the outside of our circle. The elder chants, raising his face to the sky. He lights the peace pipe, puffing smoke and blowing it in the air. The drumming continues, calling the Solstar beings to our circle. First wolf appears, then eagle, bear, snake, owl, turtle, hummingbird, and mountain lion. I hear their unified voices calling for change. The giant trees lean in, offering their support for our great endeavor. I join the chanting voices, linking my voice with the animals, trees, stars, and moon. Our unified song floats upon the wind as one voice arising from many voices.

The ceremony is ending, and I am face-to-face with the elder shaman. He gazes at me, reaches into his pouch, and sprinkles a fine red powder on my head and shoulders. "Light warrior," he declares. He presses a red dot between my eyes and lightly taps my feet and hands with his prayer stick. Drahana places her hands upon my head and solar plexus. A charge of electricity flows through my body, and my spine straightens. I stand tall and proud. I speak: "I am a light warrior!" The elder nods and continues around the circle, blessing every being. When he has completed his blessings, he rises off of the ground into the sky and disappears into the blackness of space. Drahana and I kneel to drink from the sacred indigo water. I repeat aloud, "I love you, I bless you, I love you, I bless you." The water quenches my thirst for unity, restoring my every cell. My body becomes stronger instantly, with my light warrior essence restored. Drahana motions it is time to go . . . and we rise into the sky.

Returning to the rainbow, I dive into the ocean with Stella Maris. I float on my back, taking in the grace of the present moment. I descend, sinking deeper and deeper underwater. I can breathe easily. I open my eyes. The crystal-clear water reveals a large symbol floating toward me. It is a giant, three-dimensional Vesica Pisces, taller than I am. I am encircled by the shape. The symbol extends a couple of feet above my head and below my toes. I am enveloped by the resonance of this sacred geometric shape. I rest. I receive. After some time, the Vesica Pisces disappears, and a large golden flower-of-life orb comes into view. The flower surrounds me with the pure golden rays of a thousand suns. I rest and I receive. The flower dissolves and a *Merkaba,* or creation star, emerges. It shines with violet, blue, purple, gold, and silver. A Merkaba is one of the best-known symbols of divine creation. *Mer* means "light." *Ka* means "spirit." *Ba* means "body." I am within the star. Deep peace pervades my being, as spring-green energy surrounds me. I rest and receive. The light changes to pure silver starlight. I witness my entire form fill with soft silver light.

The light shines from my heart and through my body, revealing my beautiful star form. A perfect star is made with my arms and legs. I am so beautiful!! Stella Maris surrounds me, swimming in circles. Mother Mary, Quan Yin, and Queen A'Mara appear, congratulating me on completing the final step of my journey and blessing my new beginnings ahead. Standing in my star self, I am overcome with tears of gratitude. The water being lifts me to the surface, allowing my feet to walk on the water. I raise my arms in gratitude to the Divine Mother, thanking her for the immaculate gifts. I thank Drahana for the incredible journey and affirm to Stella Maris that I will share their messages with the world. Mother Mary, Quan Yin, and Queen A'Mara hug me with love and adoration. The Stella Maris High Council dances together toward the giant rainbow and disappears.

I am on the grassy knoll, and a scroll appears in my hand. I unroll it, place my hand on my heart, and read aloud:

The Scroll of Light Leadership

Standing in the power and peace of my divinity, I proclaim:

I am an ancient wisdom keeper

I am a Light Warrior

I am a Light Leader

I bring my ancient gifts and wisdom forth to use for the benefit of all

It is the time of miracles,
where heaven is created on Earth through my "I AM" presence

I honor the indigenous people of the Earth
and acknowledge them as great and wise leaders of the new world

I support their mission as we make changes for the new Earth's family

The Solstars are working their magic

Stella Maris is always available to support me

Mother Mary, Quan Yin, and Queen A'Mara are with me
every step of the way

The Divine Mother is here

I embrace the support of the Great Spirit

We are one

I stand for what is right

My way is clear, and I follow the path of my heart and soul without fail

All of life is organizing around my greatest purpose

I live my highest divine purpose and most beautiful life

I Love You

I Bless You

My wings unfurl

My heart shines with the brilliance of a thousand stars

My courage surrounds me

Power and strength pervade my body

I gratefully meet the rising dawn of a new age

I am a Starseed Light Activator

I live my purpose and meet my destiny

I stand in my starlight divinity
Stepping into the great divine feminine revolution as Light Warrior

And so it is

Part 4
Final Reflections

Chapter 21

Blessings for Your Journey Home to Oneness

The heroic journey of writing this book was not always easy. Following my intuition was very challenging at times. Listening to the invisible voices of Stella Maris was new to me. Sometimes it was really hard, and I worried about what others would think about dolphin communication which sounded so "out there." The process of creating this book helped me to develop a greater trust in the higher realms and my own heart. I learned I could no longer give away my power to others.

One of my biggest hurdles was in believing I was a writer. I believed some people were writers, and then there were the rest of us. Once I committed to this project, I realized I could access all of the skills I needed, because I was much more powerful than I had imagined. With the help of my Higher Self, anything was possible.

When people first asked me about what I was writing, I couldn't even tell them. I would evade their questions and change the subject. Later, I began to say I was writing about dolphin wisdom, and finally I said: "Thank you for asking; I am channeling the wisdom of Stella Maris, dolphin light messengers who are here to offer their guidance and support for our healing." Boom! How is that for an answer? Many people didn't know what to say after that. Oh well, not my business. I felt liberated, as I released myself from the prison of caring what others think. I understood my path was to follow my divinely guided assignments to the best of my ability while living my happiest and most beautiful life, and all the rest was no longer my concern.

I am happy to report that many of my fears have been replaced by a deep faith. When I don't understand something, I wait patiently with wonder until the answer reveals itself. As I integrate more high vibration energy, alignment seems to occur without effort. I watch in awe at the magic and delight of it all! Sometimes I even have to pinch myself, wondering if the miracles are really happening.

I share my experience so you will know that fears and doubts are a normal part of the divine feminine path. Honor all of your experiences, especially when your critical self and left brain show up. They too can give you useful guidance. You have my full support to tell them to take a seat. Listen to the wisdom of your dreams, imagination, intuition, and visions, for they will offer you divine guidance. The divine feminine way is about living in the unknown, in the depths of creative Source energy, and I wouldn't want to live any other way.

Your Life Is a Living Prayer

Stella Maris invites you to use your life as a living prayer for the healing of yourself and the world. By anchoring yourself in the energy of light and love, you transmit this energy and light to others. This transmission is a frequency or vibration, an invisible energy signature that you emit. You are invited to actively raise your vibrational frequency. What does this mean? Anchor yourself in your Higher Self, speak your truth, and live in a way that brings more love and light into the world. It's really that simple.

You receive and emit energy all of the time, magnetizing similar frequencies to you. When you put your attention on suffering, problems, and violence, a lower vibrational energy enters your energy field. You unconsciously emit this energy back into the world. So stop doing this! As you awaken, you will become more and more responsible for the energy you allow in your life.

Stella Maris cautions you to be very careful about the vibratory energy you allow in your life. Light activators often match the lower vibrational energy of suffering, because of their great empathy. You are being called to transcend this tendency and to raise your vibration instead. You can offer the greatest help to others by standing in the light of who you are and beaming love. Raising your vibration does not mean you deny or suppress your human feelings or experience. It means you embrace your human experience and allow all of your feelings. Then the embraced emotions can pass through and be released back into the flow. Your feelings are an incredibly important guidance system for your heart. Carefully choose where you want to put your attention and energy. I invite you to live in this new way. Stella Maris invites you to cultivate your ability to rest in the light of your heart, where love and joy abound. Live the Beauty Way and step into your most creative and inspiring life.

Daily Practices

You might have many questions forming. What does this mean for daily life? And how will I live differently? Embracing the divine feminine can create higher sensitivity, and you will be more affected by both the beauty and negativity of this world. So you may have to make some changes in how you live your life.

This means changing your entertainment choices and avoiding world news, violence, and gore. You will notice that when you ingest this type of content into your energy field you may feel more depressed and anxious. Yes, this means exercising to ground higher frequencies and eating in a way that is healthful for your body. You will notice that if you eat food that is unhealthy or toxic you will feel really sick. (I can't drink alcohol anymore because it clouds my Higher Self receptors and makes my body feel bad.) Yes, this means carefully choosing who you will spend your time with. If you have toxic relationships or dysfunctional friends, you will need to set boundaries and choose to spend time with those who uplift you. Yes, this means reevaluating your entire life so you may live in higher levels of divine alignment. Perhaps you will need to change your work situation. Yes, this path involves radical responsibility and personal discipline.

Creating healthy boundaries is one important way you activate and anchor the love and light in a new way. And it is not your business what others think about it! As I set boundaries, I was able to connect more and more with the high-frequency vibrations of the universe. Every one of us has this capacity; it is just a question of whether we are willing to do the work. How much light and love are you ready to receive?

Anchoring in unity consciousness does not mean you reject or deny your human feelings. Some call feelings of anger, sadness, jealousy, or judgment the "shadow." Shadow aspects need to be embraced by the light just as much as all other aspects. Living a divine feminine path means creating space for all of your feelings and experiences. Feeling and accepting your feelings allows them to move through your mind, body, and spirit. Be brave and give your feelings space and a voice. All parts are welcome in the domain of light.

You may also have psychological parts within that are often ignored and forgotten. I now create space for all of my inner selves: my inner critic, my anger, my fear, my wounded inner child, and many others. They are still here, all of my inner parts and feelings, but I am wise enough to lean in and listen. Experiencing the storm of my difficult emotions, I allow them and listen to the guidance they bring. I trust that my human self can't always see the bigger picture, but my Higher Self can. I have faith that the Divine Mother is always conspiring for my success and happiness. Life is for me. That's what I choose to believe.

Many practices can help you to anchor new higher vibrational frequencies. Discover practices that bring you the most joy, inspiration, and peace. Learn to listen to the whispers of your heart, the Divine Mother/Cosmic Intelligence, and your helpers. For me, daily exercise, healthful eating, ceremony, praying, meditation, listening, creativity, sacred space, solitude, and time in Nature help most. Spending time in Nature recharges me and aligns me with Gaia Earth's rhythms. Nature resets the balance in my body, mind, and spirit, counteracting the influence of the modern-day world. The practice of joy and fun has transformed my life. Every day I prioritize laughter, allowing my inner child to be creative and free.

I have found the Hawaiian Ho'oponopono prayer an immensely helpful practice, so I will share it with you. There are four simple steps for this powerful healing prayer. State your challenge or issue, then say, "I'm sorry," which brings forth the power of inner responsibility. Second, say, "Please forgive me," which activates the healing power of forgiveness. Third, say, "Thank you," which brings in the power of gratitude. Fourth, say, "I love you," which initiates the divine healing power of love. This powerful prayer can be used as often as you like for any situation, within or without.

One of my other favorite practices is calling in my circle of light. I learned this practice from my mentor as a way to surround myself with heaven's help and align my free will with the divine will of my Higher Self. Sitting quietly, I take several deep breaths. With my eyes closed, I imagine my helpers and guides all around me in a circle. Isis is always in the north, Mary Magdalene in the south, Quan Yin on my left, Mother Mary on my right. Stella Maris swims in the southeast. (Every circle of light is different, so you will discover your own circle of many helpers.) At the center of my circle stand my Higher Self and the Divine Mother Source. Outside of my inner circle are other concentric circles of light beings. There is a circle of my angel team, who stand facing me, touching wing to wing. My animal soul guides are there as well:

a black panther, a hummingbird, and a unicorn. Once I envision my circle, I invite all of my helpers to guide and support me. I share my intentions, questions, and reflections with them and then listen for the answers.

The divine feminine practice of gratitude is another key to a joy-filled life. Even in difficult experiences, thankfulness can alchemize your struggles into peace. Trusting in the guidance of your Higher Self, you will know that every moment is a gift offered for your highest evolution. You can accept all circumstances with the knowledge that you have designed the perfect atmosphere of learning for yourself. I practice gratitude in many ways, through the feeling of my heart and also by using affirmations like, "I offer gratitude for _____," or "Thank you for _____."

Good news! You are the teacher you have waited for! It is all within you. Be willing to receive the knowledge from within yourself, and transcend this apparent reality through the power of love. Your light will transform the world around you, beyond your understanding and without effort! The journey begins with your willingness to heal and activate your own light first. Accept the invitation to become more of your true self. I invite you to have faith in the larger plan unfolding in your life. You are an integral key to the awakening on Earth. Unleash your magnificence, and the support of the entire universe will rise to meet you. Be the New World Imagineer you came to be! I invite you to suspend doubt, and exercise your imagination, if only for a moment. See what happens in your life as a result.

The Divine Feminine Cycle of Learning

When I run after what I think I want, my days are a furnace of stress and anxiety; if I sit in my own place of patience, what I need flows to me, and without pain. From this I understand that what I want also wants me, is looking for me and attracting me. There is a great secret here for anyone who can grasp it. —Rumi

I noticed an interesting phenomenon that occurred when I embraced a divine feminine approach to life. The divine feminine way was quite opposite to what I was taught by our masculine culture, which touts finding happiness outside of ourselves and chasing after goals. As I raised my vibration, prayed, and set intentions for what my heart wanted, my truest desires came to me. Many things came in unexplainable and easy ways. For example, when I needed to find a new editor for this book, I had no idea how to find the right person. Then a beautiful new friend had a dream about me sharing dolphin light work and wrote to tell me. I filled her in on my current challenge and she gave me the name of a great editor. How can logic explain how someone else's dream would find me an editor? It can't!

There were three phases that I cycled through when I began living the divine feminine approach to life. I hope this description of the three phases helps you as you delve into your Higher Self, embrace the divine feminine, and receive your inner wisdom.

First, there was a restoration phase, where I rested and received more of myself. It was about darn time that I took care of myself. Withdrawing from worldly activities, I spent time in solitude. In the silence of my heart, I connected with my Higher Self. I invited, listened, and observed. I watched for the signs from my guides and followed synchronicities. I meditated, walked in Nature, and engaged in other mindfulness practices that brought me fully into the present moment. Resting in oneness, I strengthened my ability to see and hear the higher realms. I wrote daily so I could record the messages I received. One of the greatest divine feminine practices I engage in is non-doing or being.

Second, I entered an active phase where I acted upon my Higher Self's guidance, taking action to bring my insights and ideas into form. In this phase, I adventured, created ceremony, traveled, engaged in creative projects, and embarked on new ventures. My divine masculine energy helped me to know the steps I needed to manifest my vision. I showed up every day to my tasks with commitment and willingness. I listened to spiritual teachings and participated in groups with friends to anchor my new consciousness. This was usually a very energetic, exciting, and active phase.

Third, there was an integration phase, where I let go of all the doing so I could integrate my new experiences and learning. I renewed my body, mind, and soul through yoga, massage, and spa days. I "beditated," a term I coined for lying in bed and meditating. I offered myself kindness and encouragement, speaking kindly to myself about how proud I was of my courage. I embraced my emotions, giving them the time and space to express themselves and be heard. I engaged the practice of gratitude, knowing all of my experiences were a gift for my divine evolution.

During my journey with Stella Maris, my self-love grew daily, and I remember at one point wrapping my arms around my body, enveloping it with so much love, I was literally falling in love with myself! What a relief after all the years of self-judgment and self-loathing, when I had forgotten who I really was. Past traumas and limiting beliefs were cleared through my connection with Stella Maris, and I became more and more whole.

Honestly, the divine feminine path is not always comfortable or easy, and I had to use every ounce of my courage and inner resources to walk in the sheer vulnerability. My willingness to grow and to face hard things unfolded into gifts of more beauty, joy, fun, and magic. It was like I was on a great treasure hunt in a garden of delightful surprises where the right people, books, and experiences appeared in my life. I embraced my divine power to create the good, beautiful, and wonderful wherever I went. And then there were the difficult human days, when I was overcome by fear or sadness. On these days, I prayed and I loved myself through it, asking for help from my angels and the Divine Mother. My journey continues to this day, as the spiral of awakening never ends.

Chapter 22

Pilgrimage to the Dolphins

The Isle of Kauai

Near the end of my writing journey, I traveled to the divine feminine island of Kauai. The indescribable beauty of this place always leaves me breathless. The scent of fresh flowers fills the humid air, and a feeling of the Divine Mother is palpable. Evidence of her incredible creativity abounds: flowering orange trees, white birds, waterfalls, geckos, and yes, even the crazy chickens. The presence of Stella Maris is so strong on Kauai; they always greet me with great joy at this sacred portal. Upon my arrival, I chose a beautiful orchid to offer as a gift from my heart to the Ocean Mother. Wading into the water, I lovingly gazed at the sea, shedding tears of gratitude for the opportunity to be in her presence.

The first night I received a lucid dream where I witnessed the unfolding of the Beauty Way, the dawning of unity consciousness on Earth. In the dream, children, women, and men planted seeds of hope in the dark soil. They danced across the Earth, with every movement creating healing through the power of love. They sowed seeds of light with trust and faith, carefully placing them in locations around the world. The seeds sprouted before my eyes, arising from the invisible love of a thousand divine hands. Flowers bloomed in every corner of the Earth, blessing and delighting life itself. They were a symbol of renewal, the dawning of spring on Earth.

I walked amongst the new flowers, receiving the beauty of their essence and diversity. Resting under a blossoming tree, I was surrounded by huge clusters of yellow and white flowers. The bees quietly buzzed a song of renewal, dissolving me into the warmth and light of spring. A resounding voice spoke: *The dawning of spring on Earth is here.* The words reverberated through my being. When I awoke, I knew the dream was real. It is just the beginning of the dawning of a new world. The power of the light will ensure that spring will come. Do not lose hope.

As the brightness of the morning light illumined my room, the beautiful voice from my dream continued:

Anchored in the light of humanity, we are initiating a great and lasting spring on Earth. Born for this noble purpose, together we will create a new day.

You are the miracles we have waited for. Let us begin our peaceful revolution on behalf of all of life on Gaia Earth. We have waited for this moment, and it is finally here.

Limahuli

On the day of the Aquarius new moon, I embarked on a sacred pilgrimage to the garden of Limahuli. This rainforest garden is anchored by the majestic Makana Mountain, with vast views of the Pacific Ocean. The garden offers a glimpse into the life of ancient times, before modern-day development on the island. The name Makana means "gift," and ancient stories say Limahuli is the place where all souls enter and leave the Earth. In my experience, this garden is a sacred portal to the spiritual realms. This place is still stewarded by Hawaiian high priestesses. The land has an otherworldly feeling, a deep silence, the pure resonance of Source.

As we parked, I noticed a lone guardian standing on the bright green Mount Makana. The guardian spoke to me in a whisper, inviting me to walk with great reverence on the holy land. I bowed my head with respect, understanding it was an honor to visit. Through the center of the garden, a fast and lively river greeted me with stunning pools and waterfalls. The sacred presence of the water being welcomed me with tender mist and rainbows.

At the top of Limahuli I sensed a vast portal of light. I stood still, taking in the vista of the valley, Mount Makana, and the Pacific Ocean. It felt like heaven on Earth. Under a nearby tree, I carefully placed my Stella Maris book and created a ceremonial altar with natural elements of stone, water, crystals, and small dolphin figures.

The new moon in Aquarius was the perfect moment for planting seeds for new beginnings. Calling in my circle of light, I prayed for world healing, unity, and awakening for Gaia Earth. I asked for blessings for the Stella Maris book, so it could reach all those who could be helped by its messages. I spoke my words out loud, using the power of my voice to activate their magic. A gust of wind blew across my body, lifting my wishes up into the sky and out to the vast blue ocean. The presence of Stella Maris became very strong, and a droplet of water landed on my forehead. In the sea, directly in front of me, whales appeared! An entire pod! They leapt in the air, breaching and spouting water. Squinting to see closer, I thought I could make out the forms of tiny dolphins as well. My Cetacean friends were joyously dancing and leaping before my eyes, and I knew this was confirmation that my prayers were received. Overwhelming love filled my heart, tears streaming down my face, and I giggled out loud. My laughter appeared to me as tiny butterflies floating on a breeze toward Mount Makana and the Ocean Mother. In my heart, I felt incredibly blessed and grateful.

My life had been forever changed by the blessings of Stella Maris. I now remembered who I was, a volunteer light activator with an important mission to fulfill. What a gift to understand my true purpose! What an honor to experience the magical Beauty Way of life. Under the darkness of the new moon, the guidance of my heart was so bright, and I knew without a shadow of a doubt that I was lovingly supported by the Divine Mother. My life was now consecrated as a living prayer of love and light.

Kealakekua Bay

Kealakekua Bay is located on the Kona coast of the Big Island of Hawaii. The name Kealakekua means "God's pathway." As I finished my first book, Stella Maris asked me to make one more sacred pilgrimage to the Big Island. Kealakekua Bay was where they wanted me to go, a place surrounded by many Heiaus, Hawaiian temples built for healing and spiritual connection. Steep cliffs overlook the bay, a burial place of Hawaiian royalty. Wild dolphins live here year-round, infusing the water with their high vibrational energy. The aqua-blue water here is like nothing I had ever experienced; crystal clear, soft to the touch, and charged with an electrical healing energy. The sacred water is tended and blessed by the dolphin 'aumakua as they glide in circles around the bay. While swimming near the cliffs, I received a vision of a sacred portal, a doorway between Earth and the higher realms. A tunnel of light where the dolphins can travel to other parts of the world and beyond.

I paddled my kayak across the bay, watching for any sign of the wild dolphins. My heart spoke to them, sending waves of love and joy. Before long, two tiny baby dolphins appeared, leaping out of the water several times. They were the cutest and smallest dolphins I had ever seen. Once again, the youngest dolphins had revealed themselves first.

I followed them into the water with ease, leaping confidently into the ocean, the fear of my first dolphin swim a distant memory. Chanting sacred sounds under the water, I invited the dolphins to come close. From the sapphire-blue depths, four figures slowly emerged. They gathered before me in a semi-circle, standing upright in the water before me. They looked at me with rapt attention, like we were having a council meeting. We gazed at each other, connecting through the joy of our hearts. I heard the words, "Thank you for listening to us and for sharing our messages with the world. We are so grateful you agreed to use your voice, heart, and hands to bring our messages to life. May our messages bless the heart of humanity and restore right relationship between our families. May you return to oneness to bring balance to our Beloved Gaia Earth. This is a new beginning, the start of a new world. We bless you always and forever. We love you."

After their final words, they rose to the surface for air and dove deep, re-joining a V formation of their pod below. Under the water, I heard a faint chant: "One family, one heart, one being, one light, one love . . . one family, one heart, one being, one light, one love," as it reverberated through the crystal blue ocean water.

Beautiful Bimini

Bimini is a small island in the Bahamas, located about 50 miles west of Florida. The crystal-clear ocean water that surrounds this narrow island is stunning, appearing in a beautiful array of aqua, sapphire blue, and green. The colors were a dream for someone like me, whose favorite color is aqua-marine. The island was a favorite place of Ernest Hemingway and Martin Luther King Jr, and mystic Edgar Cayce said it was part of the lost continent of Atlantis.

When I discovered that WildQuest, one of the only retreat centers in the world dedicated to connecting humans with wild dolphins, was in Bimini, I knew I had to visit. A small green frog accompanied me on the flight over from Ft. Lauderdale, dropped out the plane's ceiling, and landed near me. I wasn't sure if he/she was coming home or moving, but the frog's presence calmed me as I anxiously gripped my seat cushion. All I can say is that I wasn't used to flying on small chartered planes. Once we arrived safely, I stepped off the plane and was welcomed by a soft breeze charged with the feeling of freedom.

Each day, our retreat group set out on a catamaran to find the wild dolphins. The aqua water captivated me—its presence pure and inviting, infused with the frequency of dolphin consciousness. With an international group of dolphin enthusiasts, we joyously awaited finding them each day. When they appeared, we met them with incredible elation and happiness. They graciously received our joyful hearts, flipping up their pink bellies, jumping, and celebrating their awesomeness with us. The dolphins were truly as happy to see us as we were to see them.

I felt like a pro now, snorkel and fins on—check—jumping with the right timing—check—and swimming like I had a tail—double check. I relished every moment in the water with them, singing through my snorkel and bursting with love. One large Atlantic spotted dolphin joined me for a side-by-side swim. We glided next to each other like old friends, his eyes wise and eternal . . . ancient in fact . . . just like Theseus.

The clarity of the water was incredible; I could see down eighty feet or more. I witnessed the existence of a large, crystalline city where many higher realm beings reside. They live just out of view from physical eyes, existing in high vibrational reality, anchoring unity consciousness and healing on Earth. There were bright purple sea fans, mystical doorways, and the presence of many mermaids and mermen. The evolved beings of oneness are still here, alive and well, even after all this time.

During the retreat, we experienced how it felt to live as a pod of humans, a true community. It was divine! Strangers became family, elders and youngers talked about life, we celebrated life together. We were connected by our love of the Cetaceans. One pod, one world in action. This is the new way, uniting as one family, one heart, one love. This is our divine birthright. The Stella Maris book was blessed once more by the dolphins of Bimini, and I knew it was time to share their messages with the world.

I will keep swimming with wild dolphins for the rest of my life. The experience can't be captured in words and is life-changing every time. Good news: My husband and children are all on board, so I have company for the many adventures to come. Maybe someday you will join me!

An Invitation and Blessing:
Until We Meet Again

Dear Reader:

You have made it to the end! Or shall we say the beginning? Here is your jumping-off place, where you decide if you will dive into the depths of oneness and embrace a new way of living your divinity. The Beauty Way invitation awaits your free will choice. It is just that simple. Beware: You may experience the side effects of uncontrollable laughter, fun, joy, and imagination. Take time to integrate all the teachings offered here. Rest, restore, and receive. Connect to Stella Maris as often as you like, for they are here to support and guide you always. Repeat the journeys and activations. Open to a random page and see which dolphin is supporting you. Keep this book close, for it radiates love and light to your heart at all times. I hope you will join us for the great work ahead. Let us find each other with ease, so that all of the light activators can work in unison for the greatest blessing of our world. Ignite your joy and live your most beautiful life.

Wherever you go, the Earth is blessed! Your presence, your light, and your heart are gifts to the world. Each and every one of you has an incredibly important role in this life. We invite you to shine your light and love, transforming the world. Listen deeply to the whisperings of your heart, and take action. Join us in holding the vision of what is possible here on Earth, and participate as a New World Imagineer, creating new paradigms, beliefs, and systems.

Countless beings rise in gratitude for your courage to step forward as a wayshower. Your beautiful gifts can be offered only by you. May your journey be easeful and full of magical surprises. May you en-joy diving into unity. Bless your life, dear one, always and forever. *A-Ju-La: We are one family, one heart, one light, one love.*

With leaping joy and starlight water blessings,

Adena and Stella Maris

Stella Maris Glossary

Aquarian Age: A term Stella Maris uses to describe the current cycle of time on Earth. The Age of Aquarius is an astrological age when the sun's position changes from the constellation Pisces to the constellation Aquarius. Each cycle takes 25,800 years to complete. We are here at the transition to the Aquarian Age. Every age has its own energetic resonance, and the Age of Aquarius is one with divine order, peace, unity, and awakening.

Ascended Masters: Spiritual teachers who lived as humans, awakened to their divine self, and after their physical death assist beings from the higher heavenly realms. Examples are Jesus, Buddha, Mother Mary, Mary Magdalene, Quan Yin, and Isis.

'Aumakua: Hawaiian word Stella Maris uses to describe themselves and their relationship to us. The word means ancient guardians or family who inspire, protect, and guide us. 'Aumakua exist simultaneously in both the higher realms and Earth, and can return in different forms.

The Beauty Way: A way of being and living that embodies your true divine self. By awakening to your unity consciousness, you live in and as beauty, bringing the sacred and beautiful to Earth through the prayer of your life, and by living anchored in the vibrational frequencies of love, joy, and light. It is a lost divine feminine path that embraces the expression of your highest creativity, sourced from oneness. The Beauty Way is now being returned to the world by the reemergence of the divine feminine teachings and light messengers like Stella Maris and Mother Mary.

Circle of Light: The guides, angels, and ascended masters who stand in a circle around you at all times, offering their help and support. They are always available to help, if you simply ask.

Crystar: A word Stella Maris uses to describe the newest generation of light activators on Earth. Stella Maris explains that Crystar beings are spiritual/high-vibrational beings who have usually not incarnated on Earth before. There are sometimes exceptions. Crystars have been born more and more since the year 2000, but there have been some forerunners. The consciousness on Earth has elevated enough to support Crystars to take form here. They hold incredible gifts that will create solutions to the challenges the world is facing.

Divine Mother: A term used to describe the one being, Source, who creates all of life. Many other words are used in our world to describe this being, such as the Source, Creator, the Divine, God, Goddess, Sophia, Creatrix, the Universe, the Universal Mother Field, and the One Being. Divine Mother sounds feminine, but Stella Maris perceives the Divine Mother as beyond a feminine or masculine form. Divine Mother is used in this book to describe the unified field of being that we are and in which we all arise. They also use the words "Source" and "Great Maha Ocean Mother" to describe the same being.

Gaia Earth: A term Stella Maris uses to describe the divine feminine being or soul of the Earth. Gaia Earth is aware, and consciously offers her earthly body as a place for other beings to embody, grow, and learn. The name Gaia comes from Greek Mythology and means "mother of all life."

Higher Realms: There are many worlds and realms that coexist with ours in different energetic frequencies. Joy and love permeate higher vibrational worlds, light is more evident, and life exists with more ease. The higher realms are like heaven or paradise, because the Source of universal love energy infuses everything at all times. The Source offers the purest love in the universe. Light messengers or angels live in this oneness at all times and can bring this love to you.

Higher Self: A term that describes the divine, eternal, omnipotent, conscious, and true self of every being. The self that always rests in unity consciousness, the one divine source. Other words that have the same meaning as Higher Self are "true self," "divine self," "authentic self," "wise self," "God self," and "heart."

Higher Vibrational Frequency or Resonance: Stella Maris uses the terms "vibrational frequency" or "vibrational resonance" to refer to the wave energy that resides within and around you. High vibrational frequency is waves of positive energy such as love, joy, and light. Ascension is the process of integrating more light into your physical form. Stella Maris speaks about ascension by using the word "awakening." As we live in more and more alignment with our Higher Self, our frequency or resonance moves up, because this part of us always exists in the higher vibrational state of unity consciousness.

Inner Child: The inner child is the inner part or psychological aspect that remains a child and holds the memories and experiences of childhood. The inner child is the aspect of you that holds the powerful gifts of joy, wonder, imagination, and magic. The inner child holds qualities that are critical to creating a new world.

Lemuria: An ancient continent that existed on Earth and was destroyed by a cataclysmic event. The beings and culture of Lemuria continue to exist in higher vibrational form. Lemuria is sometimes referred to as Mu, which means the Motherland. The people of Lemuria were highly evolved and spiritual. Many of these advanced souls have incarnated on Earth at this time to assist with awakening.

Light Activator: Stella Maris's term for light worker. Stella Maris prefers light activator instead of light worker, because it describes the activating of love and light in individual and collective consciousness. They also do not like to frame this important purpose as work, and thus have chosen to use the words "light activator." Light activators are here to activate love and light in the world through the power of their Higher Self divinity. Stella Maris refers to awakening as the process of coming into awareness of the existence of the Source as part of oneself, as a divine self-remembrance, and as self-realization. Light activators help others to remember their own divinity and to live awakened lives through the power of their "I AM" presence. This presence manifests instant healing for all life.

Light Language: The language of the Divine Mother source. All beings are fluent in this language because of their true identity as divine beings. Light language is a powerful and transcendent language that is known by the heart of every being. The language can be communicated through sacred geometry, words, sound, color, light, and high vibrational frequencies. This multidimensional language is a way the higher realms can share love, light, healing, and information.

Light Messenger: A term that describes angels in service to the Divine Mother who are here to help all beings through their messages, presence, and blessings. Light messengers can appear in both spirit and physical form.

Light Worker: Anyone who devotes their life to bringing more love and light into the world. Light workers often feel a strong draw to help heal the world and have volunteered to offer their help to all beings for their awakening and remembrance.

Luminar: A word Stella Maris uses for a second group of light activators on Earth. Luminars are evolved human beings who have returned to the Earth again and again to bring love and light through the dark ages. Ancient and wise, the Luminars have many gifts to share with the world as leaders and teachers of the new world. They are literally lighthouses who have the ability to ignite the inner light of other beings who have forgotten their true nature. Luminars often need to undergo a process of inner healing before becoming way-showers for others.

Magi: Stella Maris uses this word to describe an ancient lineage of beings who use the power of magic, divine alchemy, and manifestation to shift situations toward wholeness and peace.

New World Imagineers: This term refers to all the light activators who are here to work together to create new, beautiful ways of life on Earth through design, innovation, and creation. New World Imagineers are here to work in partnership with each other and Gaia Earth to balance, heal, and restore. They will create new realities through the power of their imagination and the gifts encoded in their beings. New World Imagineers are great visionaries who will manifest new ideas, solutions, designs, and inspiration from Nature.

Solstar: A word Stella Maris uses to describe sentient being, light activator volunteers. They remind us that there are many animals and plants that are also here to consciously heal and balance the Earth. The Solstars create balance and harmony through the power of their loving hearts and divine purpose. They are the wisdom keepers who have not forgotten their connection to the Divine Mother. Solstars hold the vibration of unity consciousness.

Starseed: Starseeds are beings that have experienced life elsewhere in the Universe, on other planets and in other places. Their soul home can be on Earth or in other star systems. Starseeds have brilliant gifts encoded in their hearts to plant and grow a new consciousness on Earth.

The New World or New Age: Stella Maris uses these terms to describe a new time on Earth when beings will awaken to their true nature, restore balance, and integrate higher vibrational realities.

About the Illustrator

Florencia Burton was born in 1983 in Bariloche, Patagonia, Argentina. She is a self-taught painter and from an early age began to create through a variety of techniques. At the age of twenty-five, she devoted herself fully to being an artist and creative.

She experienced significant evolutionary leaps in her painting through her metaphysical studies and meditation practices, and her art is inspired by her mystical connection to the universe and Nature. Florencia is intuitively guided in her painting process as she feels the shapes and colors that want to manifest. She begins her art without knowing what will appear on the page. Her visionary art reflects her inner journeys and messages from other realities. You can find out more about her work at florenciaburton.wordpress.com.

About the Author

Adena Tryon lives with her family in Ashland, Oregon. This includes her Solstar companions: three dogs, four cats, three rabbits, and a wild hummingbird family. Adena offers individual and group sessions, healing ceremonies, and sacred retreats around the world. Embracing life as a modern-day priestess, she teaches the way of the divine feminine, living her unique Beauty Way. After seventeen years of serving clients as a Licensed Clinical Social Worker, she created her own approach to healing others. She offers personal sessions with the help of Stella Maris and the higher realm beings. Adena has a Masters in Social Work from the University of Denver, a Bachelor of Arts from the University of Colorado, is a graduate of Feminine Power Mastery and a Certified SoulCollage™ Facilitator. You can find out more at adenatryon.com which features her *Live the Beauty Way* blog™, upcoming events, and Stella Maris™ visionary art in print and canvas.

CPSIA information can be obtained at www.ICGtesting.com
Printed in the USA
BVIW12n2053280917
496173BV00006B/34